A Quick-Start™ Cookbook

COOKING WITH THE BLACKSTONE
OUTDOOR *GAS* GRIDDLE

101 DELICIOUS RECIPES WITH ILLUSTRATED INSTRUCTIONS,
FROM HEALTHY HAPPY FOODIE!
(B/W EDITION)

BY
MATT JASON

HEALTHY HAPPY FOODIE PRESS
SAN FRANCISCO, CA

Editor: HHF Press

Art Direction: HHF Press

Illustrations: HHF Press

All photographs in this book © HHF Press or © Depositphotos.com

Published in the United States of America by HHF Press

268 Bush St, #3042

San Francisco, CA 94104 USA

www.HHFPress.com

ISBN: 978-1-949314-30-4

101 Popular Recipes & "How To" Instructions on **Modern Cooking Techniques.**

MODER
COOKI
TECHNIQUES

Reader Reviews

By the looks of the instructions it looks simple and easy to use.
I liked the illustrated instructions and quick start chapter!

Sabrina S.

After some grill basics, such as how to use the various buttons
and controls, I was surprised to find some "pro tips" I hadn't
thought of, and a ton of recipes that look appetizing and fun.
Nice collection!

Camilla V.

For an outdoor grill junkie like me, I found this book to have
some fantastic recipes! I also really appreciated the 10 Minute
fast start chapter — it should be in the actual manual from the
manufacturer.

Gilly A.

This book came as a gift with my new grill. I quickly realized it's
not from the manufacturer, but I like it better because it seems
more straightforward and, dare I say, more useful than the guide
that came with the grill. The recipes cover a lot of territory...I'm
pleasantly surprised.

Dave B.

Wow, this book came in handy! I had to prepare for a big BBQ
party and I found some excellent ideas that made the party a
huge success. Consider the recipes for sandwiches and desserts,
they're pretty amazing actually. Who would have thought of
making a peach and berry pizza on a grill? It's amazing!

Armand S.

Introduction

Who This Book is For

If you have just purchased, or already own, the Blackstone Flat Top Griddle, then you need this book! Here's why:

Get the Most Out of Your Blackstone Flat Top Griddle!

Illustrated instructions, a quick start guide and beyond-the-manual tips and tricks will teach you how to get the most out of your griddle so that it becomes your family's favorite way to cook outdoors.

Get a Fast Start With "10 Minute Quick-Start!"

Our illustrated "10 Minute Quick-Start" chapter will walk you through your first complete meals in under 10 minutes, so you can quickly enjoy delicious burgers, stir fries, breakfast, and more instead of spending all of your time reading instruction manuals.

Clear, Illustrated Instructions

Will make using the Blackstone Flat Top Griddle so simple you can start cooking in minutes while avoiding beginner mistakes such as wrong heat, wrong ingredients, food sticking to the griddle, etc.

Go Beyond the Instruction Manual

Our Pro tips will have you cooking like the pro's in no time. Learn the science behind perfectly grilled food so that you can confidently make the best, most nutritious outdoor meals you've ever had.

Unbiased Recommendations, Workarounds, And Pro Tips

To help you confidently make amazing meals that are perfectly tailored to your family, while avoiding common mistakes, wherever you go!

All the Recipes You'll Ever Need!

101 of the best recipes on the planet will allow you to make the classic BBQ's, lunches, and dinners you are already familiar with, as well as fun and exciting recipes which will give your family the variety they love.

Contents

Main Dishes: Seafood 93

Vegetables & Side Dishes 117

Sandwiches & Breads 137

Desserts 157

CHAPTER

1

About the
Blackstone
Flat Top Griddle

What Does It Do?

The Blackstone Flat Top Griddle provides 720 inches of professional grade griddle for your back yard or really anywhere you go. Now, you can make professional quality meals and get the same results professional chefs achieve every time you cook. Make eggs, pancakes, quesadillas, grilled cheese, steak, potatoes, teppanyaki style foods and more. The Blackstone Flat Top Griddle is designed to produce perfectly even and adjustable heat over four different cooking zones, so you can always have the exact temperature you need at a moment's notice.

The Blackstone Flat Top Griddle is made with professional grade materials and provides professional quality heat in the form of 60,000 BTU of cooking power with four independent cooking zones. This means you can carefully control everything you cook with individual controls for each zone. Eggs don't cook properly at the same temperature as a steak, and the Blackstone Griddle allows you to cook both, perfectly, at the same time.

Are you an avid camper? Do you love to tailgate before the big game? Do you like to cook at friends' houses? Well, the Blackstone Griddle allows you maximum flexibility by letting you take your griddle wherever you need to go. With minimal effort you can remove the flat top, safely fold and stow the legs, and remove the propane tank. Best of all, the griddle comes with industrial grade casters so you can roll the griddle wherever it needs to go.

Because it's built from industrial grade materials, your Blackstone Griddle will be a versatile appliance for many years to come. The frame of the griddle is built with super durable powder coated steel. The burners are made from restaurant grade stainless steel and are guaranteed to produce perfectly even and powerful heat for years to come. Once you've spent some time with your Blackstone Griddle you might even consider getting rid of your more conventional gas or charcoal grills.

Say goodbye to dirty charcoal and matches forever. Charcoal is dirty, expensive, and harmful to your health, so why are you still using it? The Blackstone Griddle uses a standard refillable propane tank which attaches to the griddle with ease. And thanks to the simple push button ignitor, starting your griddle is as easy as pushing a button.

Who Is It Good For?

Because the Blackstone Griddle is large enough to cook all the parts of a complete meal at the same time, it is perfect for families who love perfectly prepared backyard favorites like burgers, steaks, and veggies, but it's also perfect for families who love to make big breakfasts. Prepare eggs, bacon, hashbrowns, and pancakes for everyone at the same time.

Do you love to cook big meals on the go? The Blackstone Griddle is perfect for camping and tailgating because of how easy it is to transport and set up. Pack it up for your next camping trip and set it up when you want to make an amazing outdoor meal. The Griddle is also perfect for anyone who loves making fresh grilled food for a professional tailgate party. Since the Griddle easily fits in the trunk of a car, you can take it with you to the game and set it up in minutes. Impress the whole parking lot with the amazing food you make for your fellow fans.

Who Is It Not Good For?

Everyone loves food cooked in the open air, but if you don't have a large enough outdoor space in which to use the Griddle, this may not be for you. A good rule of thumb is that you can use the griddle anywhere you would use a conventional gas or charcoal grill.

A Few Cautions

Because the Blackstone Griddle uses an external propane tank, you will want to exercise caution while connecting and disconnecting the tank. Always make sure all connection points are clean and free of debris. When attaching the hose to the tank, make sure the valve is completely tight before allowing gas to flow to the griddle.

The Blackstone Griddle's stainless steel flat top produces amazing results, but because it gets very hot, you should make sure children are always supervised when near the griddle.

What Are Its Health Benefits?

Charcoal grilling has been the standard for many years, but it carries a whole host of risks. First of all, charcoal fires increase the risk of fires in your yard. That's pretty bad, but did you know that cooking with charcoal also increases your risk of cancer? The combination of charcoal, lighter fluid, and dripping fats causes a variety of compounds that are considered carcinogenic. And you're not just breathing these chemicals when you cook. They're actually coating your food! Charcoal grills also contribute to air pollution by releasing large amounts of carbon monoxide and carbon dioxide into the atmosphere. The Blackstone Griddle, on the other hand, uses no charcoal and is much safer to use.

A Brief History of Grilling

You may not be surprised to hear that grilling food is a pretty old technique. In fact, it goes back over a half a million years. Early humans found that meat cooked over fire was actually more nutritious than raw meat. The reason? Bioavailability. In short, cooking meat changes the structure of proteins and fats allowing them to be more efficiently digested and absorbed by the body. Until the 1940s grilling was mostly something that people did around campfires, but after World War II and the expansion of suburbs, the popularity of backyard grilling skyrocketed. By the 1950s the back yard BBQ was a staple of family entertaining, and it remains this way today.

Better Than Conventional Grills?

Since the invention of the burger, the debate has raged over whether a grill or a flat top griddle does the best job. While it's true that grills offer burgers a smokier flavor, does that really result in a better burger? After years of research burger experts reached the conclusion that the flat top griddle is actually superior to the grill for one simple reason: It allows the burger to cook in its own juices rather that have all of those juices fall through the grate and into the fire. The end result is a more evenly cooked, juicier, more flavorful burger.

Modern Gas Griddles

When most people think of griddles they either picture a small counter top griddle that you plug in, or a giant flat top that sits in the kitchen of a diner. Because the griddle is so perfect for cooking such a wide variety of foods, the invention of the modern gas griddle makes perfect sense. By marrying the idea of a propane grill with the cooking surface of a griddle, you get an appliance that is both versatile and portable.

2

How to Use
the Blackstone Flat Top Griddle

Setting Up the Griddle

Once you have removed the Blackstone Griddle from its packaging, be sure to consult the user manual to ensure you have all of the included parts and fasteners.

Follow the step-by-step instructions to assemble the griddle, and makes sure to place it on a level surface so that it cannot roll.

Once you have fully assembled the griddle, you can use the valve hose to attach a canister of propane.

Learning the controls

The Blackstone Griddle has easy to use controls that will have you cooking in no time.

❶ Ignition button: The battery controlled ignition button lights your griddle. Simply press, hold, and the left most burner will light.

❷ Left Burner Knob: Turn clockwise to control the heat on the left burner.

❸ Left-Center Burner Knob: Turn clockwise to increase the heat on the left-center burner.

❹ Right-Center Burner Knob: Turn clockwise to increase the heat on the right-center burner.

❺ Right Burner Knob: Turn clockwise to increase the heat on the right burner.

The grilling process

Thanks to the Blackstone Griddle you can make almost anything with amazing results. Because the griddle has four independent zones, you are free to cook different foods at different temperatures at the same time. Unlike conventional grills, this gives you far greater flexibility with one appliance.

Since the Blackstone Griddle features a heavy stainless steel cooking surface, you will need to wait a few minutes for the burners to properly heat the surface. To prevent your food from sticking, you should take the time to season your griddle before use. We'll cover the seasoning process in the Pro Tips section. Once you have finished cooking, turn the burners off one by one, and be sure to turn off the valve on the propane tank.

Workarounds

The Blackstone Griddle features an easy to use ignition system, but if you find that the ignition burner is not lighting there are several possible causes. First, check to see if the battery in the ignitor has enough power. If that is not the problem, make sure you have enough gas in the tank. Another problem may be a clogged burner or gas jet. Because food or other debris can fall into the burners, they may become clogged over time. If this is the case, remove the cooking surface and use a damp sponge to clean out the burners or gas jets.

Some users have noticed that the grease drain can allow grease to drip out of the trough and down the leg of the grill, which can cause grease to pool on the ground. In order to combat this, make sure the grease trough and the catch can are properly aligned. Misalignment can cause leaks. Also, make sure to monitor the grease level so that it does not overflow or overwhelm the grease drain. Be mindful of bits of food that may fall into the grease trough as these may also cause the grease drain to become clogged.

If you find that food sticks to the surface of the griddle, there are several causes with simple solutions. First, you may not have properly seasoned the griddle. Because the griddle does not come pre-seasoned you should be sure to do this before using. Your food may also stick because you are adding it to the griddle too soon. Since the heavy cooking surface needs a little time to heat up, make sure that it is at the proper temperature before adding food. You can do this by touching a corner or small piece of food to the griddle. If it immediately sticks, wait another few minutes. Another common cause of food sticking to the griddle, is not giving it enough time to cook. Great chefs know that you shouldn't be in a hurry to flip your food. This is because most foods undergo a chemical reaction called the Maillard reaction which creates a charred layer on the food by raising it to a certain temperature. This reaction is also responsible for what is commonly known as a "sear." Giving your food enough time to sear before flipping will ensure it does not stick.

10 Minute Quick-Start

Your First Breakfast

Since your Blackstone Griddle has four individual temperature zones you can cook a complete breakfast all at once. This is perfect for camping or for a festive weekend breakfast for the whole family. We're going to start with classic steak and eggs with a side of fried potatoes. This amazing breakfast is sure to excite the entire family.

1 Collect These Ingredients:

- 8 large eggs
- 4 tablespoons vegetable oil
- 2 russet potatoes, sliced
- 1/2 yellow onion, finely chopped
- 1/2 green pepper, diced
- 2 12 oz. sirloin steaks, about 1 inch thick
- Salt and black pepper

2 Collect These Tools:

- Tablespoon
- Paring knife
- Instant read thermometer
- Spatula

The goal of "10 Minute Quick-Start" is to walk you through making your first meal so you "learn by doing" in under 10 minutes. Once you've had a chance to get familiar with how your griddle works, you can begin experimenting with all different types of foods.

3 Follow These Steps:

1. Light your Blackstone Griddle, and set the right two burners to high and the left two burners to medium heat.

2. Slice the potatoes and vegetables and season with a pinch of salt and pepper. Season the steaks, generously, with salt and pepper.

3. Place the potatoes on the griddle and allow them to cook for approximately five minutes. Then add the onions and green peppers.

4. When the right side of the grill is hot, add the steaks and cook about three minutes per side.

5. When the steaks are nearly finished, Crack your eggs directly onto the griddle surface on the left side. The Blackstone Griddle gives you plenty of room to cook everything at once. Flip the eggs, or leave them sunny side up.

6. Use the spatula to remove the eggs from the grill and distribute among four plates. Remove the potatoes and vegetables and divide them.

7. Remove the steaks and allow them to rest for a few minutes before cutting them in half and adding to the plates with the eggs and potatoes. Make sure to turn the burners off when you're finished and turn off the gas valve.

8. And that's it! you've just made your first complete breakfast on the Blackstone Griddle.

Congratulations!

You now have a perfectly cooked breakfast for the whole family, and you have learned the basics of how to use the Blackstone Griddle!

CHAPTER

4

Pro Tips

Season the Cooking Surface

Like most high quality cooking appliances, the stainless steel cooking surface of your Blackstone Griddle needs to be properly seasoned to ensure optimal cooking results. So you may be asking, "what is seasoning?" Before non-stick coatings existed, there was only one way to make sure food didn't stick to the cooking surface. By creating a layer of burnt on oil, you will not only achieve a perfect non-stick surface, you will also protect the cooking surface from scratches and oxidation. Let's get started. First, use soap and water to thoroughly wash the cooking surface. Use a cloth to dry the surface. Next, apply a small amount of oil to the cooking surface. The best oils to use are those with a high smoke point like vegetable or canola. Use a paper towel to spread the oil evenly across the cooking surface. Turn on all four burners and set the temperature to 275°F. Wait until the oil begins to smoke and the surface begins to darken. Once it is smoking, turn off the burners and allow the griddle to cool. Repeat this process two to three more times until the entire surface is evenly dark. Now your griddle is naturally non-stick and protected from damage and rust.

Keep Your Griddle Working from Season to Season

Because you are most likely going to keep your griddle outside, you will need to make sure to do a few things before you store it and before you use it again after being stored. Before you store, make sure to disconnect the gas tank and store away from the griddle with a cap on the valve. You can also purchase a cover for the griddle to keep out insects and dust. When you are ready to start using your griddle again, make sure to check the burner area for spider webs. Webs are flammable and can cause flare ups if you do not clean them out before cooking. Check the level in your gas tank to make sure you have enough fuel to start cooking. Once the tank is attached and you are ready to cook, it's a good idea to perform a new season on the cooking surface. Simply follow the instructions above and your griddle will be good as new.

The Best Way to Clean Your Griddle

After each use you will want to clean your griddle, but your griddle should not be cleaned like regular pots and pans. Since you want to build up a nice coating of seasoning to protect your griddle and get the best possible results, you need to make sure not to use things like dish soap to clean the cooking surface. Most detergents have a grease cutting ingredient and this will eat right through your layer of seasoning. The best way to clean your griddle is the way the pros do in restaurants: with a griddle scraper and hot water. You can purchase a griddle scraper which is designed to get rid of any bits of food left behind without sacrificing the seasoning layer you've achieved. To remove things like fat or sauces, a wash with very hot water will dissolve most things, which you can then scrape away. While you don't have to season your grill after every cleaning, continuous seasoning will ensure that your griddle stays dark and shiny.

Invest In the Proper Tools

Since the Blackstone Griddle is a professional grade piece of equipment, you should have professional grade cooking tools to get the most out of it. While you may have an array of spatulas in the kitchen, to get the best out of your griddle, we recommend buying two long metal spatulas. These spatulas are not only durable, they allow you to transport and flip a large amount of food at the same time. They are also thin and flexible so you can scoop up things like a whole hashbrown without dropping anything. Also recommended are at least one pair of long handled metal tongs which will allow you to reach anywhere on the griddle without worrying about getting burned.

Try Different Cooking Fats

Unlike a traditional grill which allows any cooking fat to fall onto the coals or gas jets, the Blackstone Griddle keeps your cooking fat right where you want it: on your food! Because of this, you can experiment with different flavors of cooking fat to optimize your results. Different oils impart different flavors, but they also work differently from each other. Olive oil imparts a robust and sometimes spicy black pepper flavor that gives an extra richness to food. The problem with olive oil, however, is that is has a pretty low smoke point, which means that over a certain temperature, the oil will start to taste burned. Use olive oil for foods you are cooking at lower to medium temperature, but avoid it for foods cooked over high heat. If you're looking for oil for high heat cooking, try canola or regular vegetable oil. They will allow you to cook to high heats without that unpleasant burnt taste. And of course, butter packs more flavor than almost anything, but

it also has a tendency to burn; so use butter for low heat cooking or for foods you plan to cook quickly.

The Ultimate Burger

For centuries, mankind has quested after the perfect burger. Since its invention, burger chefs have argued about the best way to grind it; the best way to form the patties; and of course... the best way to cook it. Some say you have to use fancy waygu beef imported from Japan, some say the best method is high heat over charcoal. Well, we're going to put the debate to rest once and for all. The first key to the best burger you've ever had is fat content. If you go to your local supermarket you usually have a choice between 20 percent fat or 10 percent fat. For the perfect burger, this will not do. The perfect burger has between 25 and 30 percent fat, and the best way to achieve this is to grind it yourself using a combination of chuck and short rib. If you don't feel like doing this at home, talk to your local butcher and tell them that you need ground beef with a higher fat content. Also, but sure to always use freshly ground beef. The longer it's sitting in packaging the more compressed it's getting, and compressed beef is the enemy of the perfect burger.

Once you have the right beef, form it into loose balls about 1/3 of a pound. Don't work it too much, and don't press it together, as you want the balls to just barely hold together. Light your griddle and turn the burners to medium heat. You might think that burgers cook best at high heat, but this is wrong. You want to give your burgers time to let their fat render and develop a nice flavorful sear. If you cook too fast you'll end up with overcooked burgers that are chewy inside. Drizzle a little vegetable oil on the griddle and place the ball on the griddle. Using a grill weight, press down to "smash" the burger as flat as you'd like. Don't reshape it, just let it press onto the griddle and sprinkle with salt. Use your thumb to make an indentation in the center of the burger so that it stays flat. When the first side has developed a nice sear, flip, season with salt and cook for an equal amount of time. This way your burger will have the time to render it's fat and reabsorb it as it cooks. When you've reached the temperature you prefer, remove it from the griddle and allow it to rest for five minutes. Top it however you'd like and enjoy what will be the best burger you've ever had.

CHAPTER

5

Main Dishes:
Poultry

Grilled Sweet Chili
Lime Chicken

Sweet and citrus marinated chicken is the perfect way to get some good use out of your Blackstone Outdoor Griddle. Pair this citrus sweet medley with grilled vegetables and brown rice for a quick weeknight meal.

Servings: 4
Prep time: 35 minutes
Cook time: 15 minutes

½ cup sweet chili sauce

¼ cup soy sauce

1 teaspoon mirin

1 teaspoon orange juice, fresh squeezed

1 teaspoon orange marmalade

2 tablespoons lime juice

1 tablespoon brown sugar

1 clove garlic, minced

4 boneless, skinless chicken breasts

Sesame seeds, for garnish

1. Whisk sweet chili sauce, soy sauce, mirin, orange marmalade, lime and orange juice, brown sugar, and minced garlic together in a small mixing bowl.

2. Set aside ¼ cup of the sauce.

3. Toss chicken in sauce to coat and marinate 30 minutes.

4. Preheat your griddle to medium heat.

5. Put the chicken on the grill and grill each side for 7 minutes.

6. Baste the cooked chicken with remaining marinade and garnish with sesame seeds to serve with your favourite sides.

Nutrition

Calories: 380, Sodium: 1274mg, Dietary Fiber: 0.5g, Fat: 12g, Carbs:19.7g, Protein: 43.8g.

A Quick-Start™ Cookbook: COOKING WITH THE BLACKSTONE OUTDOOR GAS GRIDDLE

Fiery Italian
Chicken Skewers

Fire up some yummy chicken skewers on your Blackstone Outdoor Griddle and really shake things up for lunch or dinner. You'll love how easy it is to make these perfectly seasoned skewers any day of the week.

Servings: 2 -4
Prep time: 1 hour 20 minutes
Cook time: 20 minutes

10 boneless, skinless chicken thighs, cut into chunks

1 large red onion, cut into wedges

1 large red pepper, stemmed, seeded, and cut into chunks

For the marinade:

1/3 cup toasted pine nuts

1 1/2 cups sliced roasted red peppers

5 hot cherry peppers, stemmed and seeded, or to taste

1 cup packed fresh basil leaves, plus more to serve

4 cloves garlic, peeled

1/4 cup grated Parmesan cheese

1 tablespoon paprika

extra virgin olive oil, as needed

1. Combine the toasted pine nuts, roasted red peppers, hot cherry peppers, basil, garlic, Parmesan, and paprika in a food processor or blender and process until well-combined.

2. Add in olive oil until the pesto reaches a thin consistency in order to coat the chicken as a marinade.

3. Transfer half of the pesto to a large sealable plastic bag, and reserve the other half for serving.

4. Add the chicken thigh chunks to the bag of pesto, seal, and massage the bag to coat the chicken.

5. Refrigerate for 1 hour.

6. Preheat griddle to medium-high heat and brush with olive oil.

7. Thread the chicken cubes, red onion, and red pepper onto metal skewers.

8. Brush the chicken with the reserved pesto.

9. Grill until the chicken reaches an internal temperature of 165°F; about 5 minutes per side. Serve warm with your favorite salad or vegetables!

Nutrition

Calories: 945, Sodium: 798mg, Dietary Fiber: 3.2g, Fat: 46.7g, Carbs: 14.7g, Protein: 112.2g.

Chipotle Adobo
Chicken

Smoky sweet chipotle peppers in adobo sauce make for one delicious marinade! Perfect served with yellow Mexican rice or cheese enchiladas for one hearty Mexican inspired meal.

Servings: 4 - 6
Prep Time: 1 - 24 hours
Cook Time: 20 minutes

2 lbs chicken thighs or breasts (boneless, skinless)

For the marinade:

¼ cup olive oil

2 chipotle peppers, in adobo sauce, plus 1 teaspoon adobo sauce from the can

1 tablespoon garlic, minced

1 shallot, finely chopped

1 ½ tablespoons cumin

1 tablespoon cilantro, super-finely chopped or dried

2 teaspoons chili powder

1 teaspoon dried oregano

1/2 teaspoon salt

Fresh limes, garnish

Cilantro, garnish

1. Preheat grill to medium-high.

2. Add marinade ingredients to a food processor or blender and pulse into a paste.

3. Add the chicken and marinade to a sealable plastic bag and massage to coat well.

4. Place in the refrigerator for 1 hour to 24 hours before grilling.

5. Grill chicken for 7 minutes, turn and grill and additional 7 minutes; or until good grill marks appear.

6. Turn heat to low and continue to grill until chicken is cooked through and internal temperature reaches 165°F.

7. Remove chicken from grill and allow to rest 5 to 10 minutes before serving.

8. Garnish with a squeeze of fresh lime and a sprinkle of cilantro to serve.

Nutrition

Calories: 561, Sodium: 431mg, Dietary Fiber: 0.3g, Fat: 23.8g, Carbs: 18.7g, Protein: 65.9g.

Honey-Lime
Marinated Chicken

Whip up something super-quick and easy for family dinner night. This is one delicious chicken recipe the whole family will love. Serve this delicious chicken with a side of grilled romaine or your favorite vegetables.

Servings: 4
Prep time: 8 - 24 hours
Cook time: 20 minutes

2 lbs. boneless, skinless chicken thighs

For the marinade:

1/4 cup fresh lime juice
2 teaspoon lime zest
1/4 cup honey
2 tablespoons olive oil
1 tablespoon balsamic vinegar
1/2 teaspoon sea salt
1/2 teaspoon black pepper
2 garlic cloves, minced
1/4 teaspoon onion powder

1. Whisk together marinade ingredients in a large mixing bowl; reserve 2 tablespoons of the marinade for grilling.

2. Add chicken and marinade to a sealable plastic bag and marinate 8 hours or overnight in the refrigerator.

3. Preheat grill to medium high heat and brush lightly with olive oil.

4. Place chicken on grill and cook 8 minutes per side.

5. Baste each side of chicken with reserved marinade during the last few minutes of cooking; chicken is done when the internal temperature reaches 165°F.

6. Plate chicken, tent with foil, and allow to rest for 5 minutes.

7. Serve and enjoy!

Nutrition

Calories: 381, Sodium: 337mg, Dietary Fiber: 1.1g, Fat: 20.2g, Carbs: 4.7g, Protein: 44.7g.

Honey Balsamic
Marinated Chicken

Sweet honey meets balsamic vinegar for a delicious marinated chicken that is perfect for your Blackstone Outdoor Griddle. Perfect served with your favorite sides or on a fluffy bed of brown rice.

Servings: 4
Prep time: 30 minutes - 4 hours
Cook time: 20 minutes

2 lbs. boneless, skinless chicken thighs
1 teaspoon olive oil
1/2 teaspoon sea salt
1/4 teaspoon black pepper
1/2 teaspoon paprika
3/4 teaspoon onion powder

For the Marinade:

2 tablespoons honey
2 tablespoons balsamic vinegar
2 tablespoons tomato paste
1 teaspoon garlic, minced

1. Add chicken, olive oil, salt, black pepper, paprika, and onion powder to a sealable plastic bag. Seal and toss to coat, covering chicken with spices and oil; set aside.

2. Whisk together balsamic vinegar, tomato paste, garlic, and honey.

3. Divide the marinade in half. Add one half to the bag of chicken and store the other half in a sealed container in the refrigerator.

4. Seal the bag and toss chicken to coat. Refrigerate for 30 minutes to 4 hours.

5. Preheat a grill to medium-high.

6. Discard bag and marinade. Add chicken to the grill and cook 7 minutes per side or until juices run clear and a meat thermometer reads 165°F.

7. During last minute of cooking, brush remaining marinade on top of the chicken thighs.

8. Serve immediately.

Nutrition

Calories: 485, Sodium: 438mg, Dietary Fiber: 0.5g, Fat: 18.1g, Carbs: 11g, Protein: 66.1g.

California
Grilled Chicken

Classic, ripe, and fresh California ingredients transform ordinary chicken into one scrumptious meal.

Servings: 4
Prep time: 35 minutes
Cook time: 20 minutes

4 boneless, skinless chicken breasts

3/4 cup balsamic vinegar

2 tablespoons extra virgin olive oil

1 tablespoon honey

1 teaspoon oregano

1 teaspoon basil

1 teaspoon garlic powder

For garnish:

Sea salt

Black pepper, fresh ground

4 slices fresh mozzarella cheese

4 slices avocado

4 slices beefsteak tomato

Balsamic glaze, for drizzling

1. Whisk together balsamic vinegar, honey, olive oil, oregano, basil and garlic powder in a large mixing bowl.

2. Add chicken to coat and marinate for 30 minutes in the refrigerator.

3. Preheat grill to medium-high. Grill chicken for 7 minutes per side, or until a meat thermometer reaches 165°F.

4. Top each chicken breast with mozzarella, avocado, and tomato and tent with foil on the grill to melt for 2 minutes.

5. Garnish with a drizzle of balsamic glaze, and a pinch of sea salt and black pepper.

Nutrition

Calories: 883, Sodium: 449mg, Dietary Fiber: 15.2g, Fat: 62.1g, Carbs: 29.8g, Protein: 55.3g.

Salsa Verde
Marinated Chicken

Spicy salsa verde is the perfect complement to savory grilled chicken. When you want to spice things up on the grill, this is just the recipe to help you add some spice to your life!

Servings: 6
Prep time: 4 hrs 35 minutes
Cook time: 4 hrs 50 minutes

6 boneless, skinless chicken breasts

1 tablespoon olive oil

1 teaspoon sea salt

1 teaspoon chili powder

1 teaspoon ground cumin

1 teaspoon garlic powder

For the salsa verde marinade:

3 teaspoons garlic, minced

1 small onion, chopped

6 tomatillos, husked, rinsed and chopped

1 medium jalapeño pepper, cut in half, seeded

¼ cup fresh cilantro, chopped

½ teaspoon sugar or sugar substitute

1. Add salsa verde marinade ingredients to a food processor and pulse until smooth.

2. Mix sea salt, chili powder, cumin, and garlic powder together in a small mixing bowl. Season chicken breasts with olive oil and seasoning mix, and lay in glass baking dish.

3. Spread a tablespoon of salsa verde marinade over each chicken breast to cover; reserve remaining salsa for serving.

4. Cover dish with plastic wrap and refrigerate for 4 hours.

5. Preheat grill to medium-high and brush with olive oil.

6. Add chicken to grill and cook 7 minutes per side or until juices run clear and a meat thermometer reads 165°F.

7. Serve each with additional salsa verde and enjoy!

Nutrition

Calories: 321, Sodium: 444mg, Dietary Fiber: 1.3g, Fat: 13.7g, Carbs: 4.8g, Protein: 43g.

Hawaiian Chicken
Skewers

Grill up a taste of Hawaii with these delicious chicken skewers! Super-easy to make, you can enjoy these yummy skewers any night of the week - just prep them a day before grilling for one easy dinner in no time.

Servings: 4 - 5
Prep Time: 1 hr 10 minutes
Cook Time: 15 minutes

1 lb. boneless, skinless chicken breast, cut into 1 ½ inch cubes

3 cups pineapple, cut into 1 ½ inch cubes

2 large green peppers, cut into 1 ½ inch pieces

1 large red onion, cut into 1 ½ inch pieces

2 tablespoons olive oil, to coat veggies

For the marinade:

1/3 cup tomato paste

1/3 cup brown sugar, packed

1/3 cup soy sauce

1/4 cup pineapple juice

2 tablespoons olive oil

1 1/2 tablespoon mirin or rice wine vinegar

4 teaspoons garlic cloves, minced

1 tablespoon ginger, minced

1/2 teaspoon sesame oil

Pinch of sea salt

Pinch of ground black pepper

10 wooden skewers, for assembly

1. Combine marinade ingredients in a mixing bowl until smooth. Reserve a 1/2 cup of the marinade in the refrigerator.

2. Add chicken and remaining marinade to a sealable plastic bag and refrigerate for 1 hour.

3. Soak 10 wooden skewer sticks in water for 1 hour.

4. Preheat the grill to medium heat.

5. Add red onion, bell pepper and pineapple to a mixing bowl with 2 tablespoons olive oil and toss to coat.

6. Thread red onion, bell pepper, pineapple and chicken onto the skewers until all of the chicken has been used.

7. Place skewers on grill and grab your reserved marinade from the refrigerator; grill for 5 minutes then brush with remaining marinade and rotate.

8. Brush again with marinade and grill about 5 additional minutes or until chicken reads 165°F on a meat thermometer.

9. Serve warm.

Nutrition

Calories: 311, Sodium: 1116mg, Dietary Fiber: 4.2g, Fat: 8.8g, Carbs: 38.1g, Protein: 22.8g.

Classic BBQ
Chicken

BBQ Chicken has never tasted so good! We love this classic BBQ favorite for a taste of summer all year around. Simply serve with your favorite side dishes for a full family style meal.

Servings: 4 - 6
Prep time: 5 minutes
Cook time: 1 hour 45 minutes

4 pounds of your favorite chicken, including legs, thighs, wings, and breasts, skin-on

Salt

Olive oil

1 cup barbecue sauce, like Hickory Mesquite or homemade

1. Rub the chicken with olive oil and salt.
2. Preheat the griddle to high heat.
3. Sear chicken skin side down on the grill for 5-10 minutes.
4. Turn the griddle down to medium low heat, tent with foil and cook for 30 minutes.
5. Turn chicken and baste with barbecue sauce.
6. Cover the chicken again and allow to cook for another 20 minutes.
7. Baste, cover and cook again for 30 minutes; repeat basting and turning during this time.
8. The chicken is done when the internal temperature of the chicken pieces are 165°F and juices run clear.
9. Baste with more barbecue sauce to serve!

Nutrition
Calories: 539, Sodium: 684mg, Dietary Fiber: 0.3g, Fat: 11.6g, Carbs: 15.1g, Protein: 87.6g.

Chicken Wings
with Sweet Red Chili and Peach Glaze

Whip up delicious, restaurant style chicken wings right at home with your Blackstone Outdoor Griddle. Sweet and savory, these chicken wings are the perfect treat for any game day or Sunday Funday with the family.

Servings: 4
Prep time: 15 minutes
Cook time: 30 minutes

1 (12 oz.) jar peach preserves
1 cup sweet red chili sauce
1 teaspoon lime juice
1 tablespoon fresh cilantro, minced
1 (2-1/2 lb.) bag chicken wing sections
Non-stick cooking spray

1. Mix preserves, red chili sauce, lime juice and cilantro in mixing bowl. Divide in half, and place one half aside for serving.

2. Preheat griddle to medium heat and spray with non-stick cooking spray.

3. Grill wings for 25 minutes turning several times until juices run clear.

4. Remove wings from grill, toss in a bowl to coat wings with remaining glaze.

5. Return wings to grill and cook for an additional 3 to 5 minutes turning once.

6. Serve warm with your favourite dips and side dishes!

Nutrition

Calories: 790, Sodium: 643mg, Dietary Fiber: 1g, Fat: 16.9g, Carbs:87.5g, Protein: 66g.

A Quick-Start™ Cookbook: COOKING WITH THE BLACKSTONE OUTDOOR GAS GRIDDLE

Chicken Tacos
with Avocado Crema

The perfect way to do lunch prep on a Sunday, you can whip this recipe up in no time and eat it for lunch all week. The whole family will enjoy these delicious tacos! Just keep your avocado crema in a sealable container until ready to assemble and you have easy healthy meals all week long.

Servings: 4-5
Prep Time: 1 hour 5 minutes
Cook Time: 10 minutes

1 1/2 lbs. Boneless, skinless chicken breasts, sliced thin

For the chicken marinade:

1 serrano pepper, minced
2 teaspoons garlic, minced
1 lime, juiced
1 teaspoon ground cumin
1/3 cup olive oil
Sea salt, to taste
Black pepper, to taste

For the avocado crema:

1 cup sour cream
2 teaspoons lime juice
1 teaspoon lime zest
1 serrano pepper, diced and seeded
1 clove garlic, minced
1 large hass avocado

For the garnish:

1/2 cup queso fresco, crumbled
2 teaspoons cilantro, chopped
1 lime sliced into wedges
10 corn tortillas

1. Mix chicken marinade together in a sealable plastic bag. Add chicken and toss to coat well.

2. Marinate for 1 hour in the refrigerator.

3. Combine avocado crema ingredients in a food processor or blender and pulse until smooth.

4. Cover and refrigerate until you are ready to assemble tacos.

5. Preheat griddle to medium heat and grill chicken for 5 minutes per side; rotating and turning as needed.

6. Remove from griddle and tent loosely with aluminum foil. Allow chicken to rest 5 minutes.

7. Serve with warm tortillas, a dollop of avocado crema, queso fresco, cilantro and lime wedges.

8. To meal prep: simply divide chicken into individual portion containers with a serving of the garnish, and take with tortillas wrapped in parchment paper to warm in a microwave to serve.

Nutrition

Calories: 703, Sodium: 357mg, Dietary Fiber: 6.3g, Fat: 44.5g, Carbs:30.5g, Protein: 47.9g.

Kale Caesar Salad
with Grilled Chicken

Light and airy, Caesar Salad is delicious tossed with grilled chicken and kale. You'll love this easy recipe that cooks up in no time - so you can enjoy healthy meals every day of the week!

Servings: 1
Prep time: 10 minutes
Cook time: 8 minutes

1 chicken breast
1 teaspoon garlic powder
½ teaspoon black pepper
½ teaspoon sea salt
2 kale leaves, chopped
shaved parmesan, for serving

For the dressing:

1 tablespoon mayonnaise
1/2 tablespoon dijon mustard
½ teaspoon garlic powder
1/2 teaspoon worcestershire sauce
1/4 lemon, juice of (or 1/2 a small lime)
¼ teaspoon anchovy paste
Pinch of sea salt
Pinch of black pepper

1. Mix garlic powder, black pepper, and sea salt in a small mixing bowl. Coat chicken with seasoning mix.
2. Preheat griddle to medium-high heat.
3. Grill chicken on each side for 7 minutes or until a meat thermometer reads 165°F when inserted in the thickest part of the breast.
4. Whisk all of the dressing ingredients together.
5. Plate your kale and pour the dressing over, and toss to combine.
6. Cut the grilled chicken on a diagonal and place on top of the salad. Garnish with shaved parmesan, and serve.

Nutrition

Calories: 643, Sodium: 1549mg, Dietary Fiber: 3.8g, Fat: 18.6g, Carbs: 26.3g, Protein: 93.3g.

Hasselback
Stuffed Chicken

Who doesn't love chicken breast seasoned to perfection and grilled like hasselback potatoes? This delicious recipe is gluten-free and diabetic friendly for one delicious dinner that you can serve with salad or steamed veggies.

Servings: 4
Prep time: 15 minutes
Cook time: 30 minutes

4 boneless, skinless chicken breasts

2 tablespoons olive oil

2 tablespoons taco seasoning

1/2 red, yellow and green pepper, very thinly sliced

1 small red onion, very thinly sliced

1/2 cup Mexican shredded cheese

Guacamole, for serving

Sour cream, for serving

Salsa, for serving

1. Preheat griddle to med-high.

2. Cut thin horizontal cuts across each chicken breast; like you would hasselback potatoes.

3. Rub chicken evenly with olive oil and taco seasoning.

4. Add a mixture of bell peppers and red onions to each cut, and place the breasts on the grill.

5. Cook chicken for 15 minutes.

6. Remove and top with cheese.

7. Tent loosely with foil and Grill another 5 minutes, until cheese is melted.

8. Remove from grill and top with guacamole, sour cream and salsa. Serve alongside your favorite side dishes!

Nutrition

Calories: 643 , Sodium: 549mg, Dietary Fiber: 3.8g, Fat: 18.6g, Carbs: 26.3g, Protein: 93.3g.

Creole Chicken
Stuffed with Cheese & Peppers

Nothing beats a grilled stuffed chicken breast that preps in 10 minutes. This easy to assemble recipe will have your family eating healthy even on busy weeknights!

Serving Size: 4
Prep time: 10 minutes
Cook time: 20 minutes

4 boneless, skinless chicken breasts

8 mini sweet peppers, sliced thin and seeded

2 slices pepper jack cheese, cut in half

2 slices colby jack cheese, cut in half

1 tablespoon creole seasoning, like Emeril's

1 teaspoon black pepper

1 teaspoon garlic powder

1 teaspoon onion powder

4 teaspoons olive oil, separated

Toothpicks

1. Rinse chicken and pat dry.

2. Mix creole seasoning, pepper, garlic powder, and onion powder together in a small mixing bowl and set aside.

3. Cut a slit on the side of each chicken breast; be careful not to cut all the way through the chicken.

4. Rub each breast with 1 teaspoon each of olive oil.

5. Rub each chicken breast with seasoning mix and coat evenly.

6. Stuff each breast of chicken with 1 half pepper jack cheese slice, 1 half colby cheese slice, and a handful of pepper slices.

7. Secure chicken shut with 4 or 5 toothpicks.

8. Preheat the griddle to medium-high and cook chicken for 8 minutes per side; or until chicken reaches an internal temperature of 165°F.

9. Allow chicken to rest for 5 minutes, remove toothpicks, and serve.

Nutrition

Calories: 509, Sodium: 1117mg, Dietary Fiber: 3.4g, Fat: 25.1g, Carbs: 19.8g, Protein: 51.4g.

Teriyaki Chicken
with Veggie Rice Bowls

Rice bowls are both delicious and nutritious and a perfect way to meal prep on a Sunday for the whole week. This recipe will keep in your refrigerator for up to 4 days once cooked and makes for a delicious meal at work or school when microwaved!

Servings: 4
Prep time: 8 hrs 10 minutes
Cook time: 20 minutes

1 bag brown rice

For the skewers:

2 boneless skinless chicken breasts, cubed

1 red onion, quartered

1 red pepper, cut into cube slices

1 green pepper, cut into cube slices

1/2 pineapple, cut into cubes

For the marinade:

1/4 cup light soy sauce

1/4 cup sesame oil

1 tablespoon ginger, fresh grated

1 garlic clove, crushed

1/2 lime, juiced

1. Whisk the marinade ingredients together in a small mixing bowl.
2. Add chicken and marinade to a resealable plastic bag, seal and toss well to coat.
3. Refrigerate for one hour or overnight.
4. Prepare rice as instructed on the bag.
5. Preheat the griddle to medium-high heat.
6. Thread the chicken and the cubed veggies onto 8 metal skewers and grill for 8 minutes on each side until charred and cooked through.
7. Portion rice out into bowls and top with two skewers each, and enjoy!

Nutrition

Calories: 477, Sodium: 362mg, Dietary Fiber: 3.8g, Fat: 20.6g, Carbs:48.1g, Protein: 26.1g.

Yellow Curry
Chicken Wings

Warm and savory, these grilled chicken wings are sure to spice things up with a taste of India. Curry Grilled Chicken Wings are best served with poppadoms, chutney, and raita dip for a delicious party snack.

Servings: 6
Prep time: 35 minutes
Cook time: 30 minutes to 1 hr

2 lbs. chicken wings

For the marinade:

1/2 cup Greek yogurt, plain
1 tablespoon mild yellow curry powder
1 tablespoon olive oil
½ teaspoon sea salt
½ teaspoon black pepper
1 teaspoon red chili flakes

1. Rinse and pat wings dry with paper towels.
2. Whisk marinade ingredients together in a large mixing bowl until well-combined.
3. Add wings to bowl and toss to coat.
4. Cover bowl with plastic wrap and chill in the refrigerator for 30 minutes.
5. Prepare one side of the griddle for medium heat and the other side on medium-high.
6. Working in batches, grill wings over medium heat, turning occasionally, until skin starts to brown; about 12 minutes.
7. Move wings to medium-high area of griddle for 5 minutes on each side to char until cooked through; meat thermometer should register 165°F when touching the bone.
8. Transfer wings to a platter and serve warm.

Nutrition

Calories: 324, Sodium: 292mg, Dietary Fiber: 0.4g, Fat: 14g, Carbs:1.4g, Protein: 45.6g.

Korean Chicken Wings
with Scallion

Grilled chicken wings are perfect when seasoned with the spice of Go-chujang. This recipe pairs perfect with a Japanese White Sauce or cool, creamy sour cream infused with lime zest. Serve them up for your next tailgate or dinner party for something elevated and fun.

Servings: 6
Prep time: 30 minutes
Cook time: 30 minutes to 1 hr

2 pounds chicken wings (flats and drumettes attached or separated)

For the marinade:

1 tablespoon olive oil

1 teaspoon sea salt, plus more

1/2 teaspoon black pepper

1/2 cup gochujang, Korean hot pepper paste

1 scallion, thinly sliced, for garnish

1. Rinse and pat wings dry with paper towels.
2. Whisk marinade ingredients together in a large mixing bowl until well-combined.
3. Add wings to bowl and toss to coat.
4. Cover bowl with plastic wrap and chill in the refrigerator for 30 minutes.
5. Prepare one side of the griddle for medium heat and the other side on medium-high.
6. Working in batches, grill wings over medium heat, turning occasionally, until skin starts to brown; about 12 minutes.
7. Move wings to medium-high area of griddle for 5 minutes on each side to char until cooked through; meat thermometer should register 165°F when touching the bone.
8. Transfer wings to a platter, garnish with scallions, and serve warm with your favorite dipping sauces.

Nutrition

Calories: 312, Sodium: 476mg, Dietary Fiber: 0.4g, Fat: 13.5g, Carbs:1.1g, Protein: 43.9g.

Buffalo Grilled
Chicken Wings

Craving restaurant style Buffalo Wings?! You can easily whip them up right at home with this quick and easy recipe. Serve them with your favorite dips, carrots and celery for a fun treat.

Servings: 6 - 8
Prep time: 10 minutes
Cook time: 20 minutes

1 tablespoon sea salt

1 teaspoon ground black pepper

1 teaspoon garlic powder

3 lbs. chicken wings

6 tablespoons unsalted butter

1/3 cup buffalo sauce, like Moore's

1 tablespoon apple cider vinegar

1 tablespoon honey

1. Combine salt, pepper and garlic powder in a large mixing bowl.
2. Toss the wings with the seasoning mixture to coat.
3. Preheat griddle to medium heat.
4. Place the wings on the grill; make sure they are touching so the meat stays moist on the bone while grilling.
5. Flip wings every 5 minutes, for a total of 20 minutes of cooking.
6. Heat the butter, buffalo sauce, vinegar and honey in a saucepan over low heat; whisk to combine well.
7. Add wings to a large mixing bowl, toss the wings with the sauce to coat.
8. Turn griddle up to medium high and place wings back on the grill until the skins crisp; about 1 to 2 minutes per side.
9. Add wings back into the bowl with the sauce and toss to serve.

Nutrition

Calories: 410, Sodium: 950mg, Dietary Fiber: 0.2g, Fat: 21.3g, Carbs: 2.7g, Protein: 49.4g.

Poppyseed Chicken
Summer Salad

Grilled Chicken Summer Salads are a refreshing and delicious way to enjoy your Blackstone Outdoor Griddle Station! Pair it with a cool, crisp glass of lemonade or sparkling water - and you've got one delicious meal.

Servings: 3
Prep time: 5 minutes
Cook time: 25 minute

3 boneless chicken breast halves

1/4 cup poppy seed dressing, plus ½ cup for basting chicken

1 bag (8 oz.) romaine salad

1 cup fresh blueberries, rinsed

1 cup strawberries, sliced

1/4 cup almonds, sliced

Sea salt, for seasoning

Black pepper, for seasoning

1. Baste chicken with ½ cup poppyseed dressing. Season each chicken breast with a pinch of pepper and sea salt.

2. Preheat griddle to medium heat.

3. Grill chicken for 10 minutes on each side or until chicken is no longer pink in center; brushing occasionally with more poppyseed dressing.

4. Let chicken rest for five minutes.

5. Toss lettuce mix with remaining ¼ cup of dressing.

6. Portion salad evenly into three bowls and top each with an even amount of blueberries and strawberries.

7. Cut chicken crosswise into ½ inch thick slices.

8. Arrange one sliced chicken breast on each salad bowl and sprinkle almonds to serve.

Nutrition

Calories: 479, Sodium: 405mg, Dietary Fiber: 3.1g, Fat: 25.8g, Carbs:16.2g, Protein: 45.2g.

Lemon Ginger Chicken
with Fruit Salsa

Fruit salsa is the perfect compliment to any grilled chicken. This zesty recipe is sure to knock the socks off the ones you love for a delicious healthy weekend meal on the grill! Simply serve with grilled veggies on the side for a healthy treat.

Servings: 4
Prep time: 1 hour
Cook time: 20 minutes

4 boneless, skinless chicken breasts

For the marinade:
1/2 cup fresh lemon juice
1/2 cup soy sauce
1 tablespoon fresh ginger, minced
1 tablespoon lemon pepper seasoning
2 garlic cloves, minced

For the salsa:
1 1/2 cups pineapple, chopped
3/4 cup kiwi fruit, chopped
1/2 cup mango, chopped
1/2 cup red onion, finely chopped
2 tablespoons fresh cilantro, chopped
1 small jalapeño pepper, seeded and chopped
1 1/2 teaspoons ground cumin
1/4 teaspoon sea salt
1/8 teaspoon black pepper
½ teaspoon olive oil, more for brushing grill

1. Combine marinade ingredients in a large sealable plastic bag.
2. Add chicken to bag, seal, and toss to coat. Marinate in refrigerator for 1 hour.
3. Combine salsa ingredients in a mixing bowl and toss gently to combine. Set aside until ready to serve.
4. Preheat the grill.
5. Remove chicken from bag and discard marinade.
6. Brush griddle with olive oil and cook chicken for 7 minutes on each side or until chicken is cooked through.
7. Serve chicken topped with salsa alongside your favorite side dishes.

Nutrition

Calories: 391, Sodium: 2051mg, Dietary Fiber: 3.7g, Fat: 12.3g, Carbs:23.6g, Protein: 46.1g.

Lemon–Olive
Grilled Chicken

The bright zest of lemon brightens this grilled chicken with a delightful summer taste. Best served with salad and risotto, you can prepare this chicken in no time!

Servings: 4
Prep time: 30 minutes
Cook time: 20 minutes

1 lbs. chicken breast tenders
1 shallot, chopped

For the marinade:

1 lemon, juiced
1 teaspoon lemon zest
4 teaspoons olive oil
1/2 teaspoon sea salt
1/2 teaspoon white pepper
1 teaspoon sugar
1/4 cup white wine, like Chardonnay

1. Mix marinade ingredients together in a mixing bowl; when well combined incorporate chopped shallot and chicken to coat well.

2. Cover and marinate for 30 minutes in the refrigerator.

3. Preheat grill to medium-high. Grill chicken for 7 minutes per side, or until a meat thermometer reaches 165°F.

4. Allow chicken to rest for 5 minutes after grilling and serve with your favorite sides.

Nutrition

Calories:166, Sodium: 458mg, Dietary Fiber: 0.7g, Fat: 5.3g, Carbs:4g, Protein: 22.6g.

Chicken Thighs
with Ginger-Sesame Glaze

Ginger and sesame come together in this delicious glaze for a taste explosion. Serve this warm and sweet chicken with brown rice and your favorite vegetables for a quick, Asian-inspired meal.

Servings: 4 - 8
Prep time: 10 minutes
Cook time: 20 minutes

8 boneless, skinless chicken thighs

For the glaze:

3 tablespoons dark brown sugar

2 1/2 tablespoons soy sauce

1 tablespoon fresh garlic, minced

2 teaspoons sesame seeds

1 teaspoon fresh ginger, minced

1 teaspoon sambal oelek

1/3 cup scallions, thinly sliced

Non-stick cooking spray

1. Combine glaze ingredients in a large mixing bowl; separate and reserve half for serving.

2. Add chicken to bowl and toss to coat well.

3. Preheat the griddle to medium-high heat.

4. Coat with cooking spray.

5. Cook chicken for 6 minutes on each side or until done.

6. Transfer chicken to plates and drizzle with remaining glaze to serve.

Nutrition

Calories: 301, Sodium: 413mg, Dietary Fiber: 0.3g, Fat: 11.2g, Carbs: 4.7g, Protein: 42.9g.

Soba Noodle Chicken
with Miso Vinaigrette

Watching your carbs or gluten intake? This is the perfect meal for any night with your love or romantic evening in. Just be sure to pick soba noodles labeled gluten-free as they can often not be created equal.

Servings: 2
Prep time: 10 minutes
Cook time: 20 minutes

1 pkg gluten-free soba noodles
1 tsp black sesame seeds, for garnish
2 skinless, boneless chicken breasts, halved like cutlets
1/2 tsp freshly ground black pepper
1/4 teaspoon kosher salt

For the marinade:

2 tablespoons olive oil
1 tablespoon white miso, or soybean paste
1 tablespoon mirin
1 tablespoon soy sauce
2 teaspoons sesame oil
1 1/2 teaspoon fresh ginger, minced
1 teaspoon honey

For the veggies:

1/2 cup carrot, shredded
1 1/2 cups red cabbage, thin sliced
1/2 cup green onions, sliced
Olive oil, for brushing

1. Prepare soba noodles according to package instructions.
2. Drain; rinse with cold water and drain again. Set aside.
3. Preheat one side of the grill to medium heat and one side to medium high heat.
4. Combine marinade ingredients in a large mixing bowl.
5. Add 2 tablespoons of the marinade to a second mixing bowl and set aside.
6. Sprinkle chicken with pepper and salt, and add chicken to marinade bowl.
7. Brush griddle with olive oil.
8. Add veggies to the medium heat side and sauté for 5 minutes.
9. Add chicken to the medium high side and cook 7 minutes on each side or until done.
10. Add noodles and veggies to the reserved bowl of marinade. Toss to coat well and return to grill for 3 minutes.
11. Remove food from grill to plate, sprinkle noodles with sesame seeds, and serve warm.

Nutrition

Calories: 625, Sodium: 1512 mg, Dietary Fiber: 3.7g, Fat: 31g, Carbs: 39.8g, Protein: 49.7g.

Chicken Satay

with Almond Butter Sauce

A mouthwatering, sweet meets spicy delight - this recipe is delicious served as an appetizer for dipping or over a bed of pad Thai noodles for an Asian-inspired dish. Serve it garnished with lime wedges and crushed peanuts for something out of this world.

Servings: 4
Prep time: 2 hrs 20 minutes
Cook time: 8 minutes

1 lb. boneless, skinless chicken thighs, cut into thin strips
Olive oil, for brushing

For the marinade:
1/2 cup canned light coconut milk
1/2 lime, juiced
1 tablespoon honey
2 teaspoons soy sauce
1 1/2 teaspoons fish sauce
1/2 teaspoon red chili flakes
2 teaspoons ginger, grated
1 clove of garlic, grated
1/2 teaspoon curry powder
1/4 teaspoon ground coriander

For almond butter sauce:
1/4 cup almond butter
1/4 cup water
2 tbsp canned, light coconut milk
1 tablespoon honey
1/2 lime, juiced
1 teaspoon fish sauce
1 teaspoon fresh grated ginger
1/2 teaspoon low sodium soy sauce
1/2 teaspoon Sriracha

1. Whisk together all of the ingredients for the marinade in a medium mixing bowl.

2. Add chicken to mixing bowl and toss to coat.

3. Cover and refrigerate 2 hours or overnight.

4. Preheat griddle to medium high heat and brush with olive oil.

5. Thread the chicken strips onto metal skewers.

6. Place the chicken skewers on the prepared griddle and cook 3 minutes, rotate, and grill another 4 minutes or until the chicken is cooked through.

7. Whisk together all of the ingredients for the almond butter sauce in a small saucepan.

8. Bring the sauce to a boil on medium heat, then lower to medium low and simmer for 1 to 2 minutes or until the sauce thickens.

9. Serve chicken satay warm with the almond butter sauce and enjoy.

Nutrition

Calories: 347, Sodium: 743mg, Dietary Fiber: 1.2g, Fat: 19.7g, Carbs: 8.6g, Protein: 34.3g.

Tequila-Glazed
Grilled Chicken Thighs

Tequila-Glazed Grilled Chicken Thighs are a delicious way to serve up a quick and hearty meal any night of the week. Serve them with rice and fajita veggies or even a delicious side of black beans and grilled vegetables. No matter how you pair this chicken, it will soon become a grill favorite.

Servings: 4 - 6
Prep time: 10 minutes
Cook time: 20 minutes

6 boneless, skinless chicken thighs

For the chicken seasoning:

1 1/2 teaspoon ground cumin
1 teaspoon chili powder
3/4 teaspoon kosher salt
1/4 teaspoon chipotle chili powder

For the glaze:

3/4 cup pineapple juice
1/3 cup tequila
1/4 cup honey
2 teaspoon cornstarch
2 teaspoon water
2 teaspoon lime zest
3 tablespoon fresh lime juice
1/4 teaspoon crushed red pepper
Non-stick cooking spray

1. Preheat grill to medium-high heat using both burners. After preheating, turn the left burner off and leave the right burner on.
2. Combine the chicken seasoning in a small bowl and rub evenly over chicken.
3. Bring the pineapple juice, tequila, and honey to a boil in a small saucepan; cook until reduced to 3/4 cup; about 10 minutes.
4. Whisk cornstarch and 2 teaspoons of water in a small bowl until smooth.
5. Add cornstarch mixture to juice mixture and whisk into a boil; cook for 1 minute, stirring constantly.
6. Remove from heat and fold in red pepper, lime zest and 3 tablespoons lime juice.
7. Spray griddle with non-stick cooking spray.
8. Add chicken to grill and cook 7 minutes on each side, basting with glaze often.
9. Move the chicken over to the left burner on indirect heat. Tent with foil and cook an additional 5 minutes on each side or until done, basting occasionally.
10. Serve warm with your favorite sides.

Nutrition

Calories: 381, Sodium: 425mg, Dietary Fiber: 0.5g, Fat: 11.1g, Carbs: 19g, Protein: 42.7g.

Root Beer Can
Chicken

A take on the traditional grilled root beer can chicken, this dish is just as delicious as the whole roasted version and packed with savory sweet flavor. Believe it or not, you can enjoy this scrumptious dish with mashed potatoes, a warm beet salad, roasted brussel sprouts, and a delicious Malbec or Shiraz for one very romantic meal.

Servings: 2 -4
Prep time: 8 hrs 10 minutes
Cook time: 20 minutes

1 lbs. boneless chicken thighs
3 (12 ounce) cans root beer, like A&W
Olive oil

For the rub:

1 tablespoon garlic powder
3/4 tablespoon sea salt
1/2 tablespoon white pepper
2 teaspoons smoked paprika
2 teaspoons garlic powder
1 teaspoon dried thyme
1/8 teaspoon cayenne pepper

1. Combine rub ingredients in a bowl; reserve half in a separate air tight container until ready to grill.

2. Rub chicken thighs evenly with olive oil and coat each with some rub.

3. Lay chicken in a 13 by 9 inch baking dish. Cover with 2 cans of root beer.

4. Preheat grill to medium-high heat.

5. Discard marinade and brush grill with olive oil.

6. Gently fold remaining rub and a half of the third can of root beer in a small bowl.

7. Grill chicken for 7 minutes on each side, basting often with root beer rub mix.

8. Serve when cooked through or chicken reaches 165°F and juices run clear.

Nutrition

Calories: 363, Sodium: 1185mg, Dietary Fiber: 0.9g, Fat: 12.1g, Carbs: 29.9g, Protein: 33.4g.

Basil, Blackberry,
and Grilled Chicken Salad

A breath of fresh air, this salad will transform your healthy lifestyle into one with robust flavors! You'll love this delicious recipe with a glass of sparkling water or iced tea.

Servings: 2
Prep time: 10 minutes
Cook time: 20 minutes

2 boneless, skinless chicken breasts,

1/4 cup extra-virgin olive oil, divided

3/4 teaspoon kosher salt, divided

1/2 teaspoon black pepper, divided

2 tablespoons white balsamic vinegar

1 1/2 teaspoons honey

1 1/2 teaspoons Dijon mustard

4 cups baby spinach

2 cups fresh basil, stems removed

1/4 cup red onion, super-thinly sliced

1 punnet fresh blackberries

½ cup goat cheese, crumbled

Cooking spray

1. Preheat grill to medium-high.

2. Brush chicken with 1 tablespoon olive oil and sprinkle evenly with 1/4 teaspoon salt and 1/4 teaspoon pepper.

3. Spray grill with non-stick cooking spray, add chicken, and cook 5 minutes on each side or until the meat thermometer inserted in thickest portion registers 165°F.

4. Allow to rest for 5 minutes and cut into slices.

5. Whisk remaining 3 tablespoons oil, vinegar, honey, mustard, remaining 1/2 teaspoon salt, and remaining 1/4 teaspoon pepper together in a large mixing bowl. Add spinach, basil, and onion; toss gently to coat.

6. Divide salad evenly among 2 plates; top evenly with chicken, blackberries, and cheese to serve.

Nutrition

Calories: 607, Sodium: 1116mg, Dietary Fiber: 6,1g, Fat: 39.7g, Carbs: 16.2g, Protein: 48.3g

Honey Sriracha
Grilled Chicken Thighs

Spicy sweet chicken thighs are not only super-tasty, but super-easy to whip up even when you are pressed for time. Simply marinate overnight and throw them on the grill after work for a quick and easy restaurant quality meal right at home.

Servings: 6
Prep: 5 minutes
Cook time: 35 minutes

2.5 lbs. boneless chicken thighs

3 tablespoons butter, unsalted

1 tablespoon fresh ginger, minced

2 garlic cloves, minced

1/4 teaspoon smoked paprika

1/4 teaspoon chili powder

4 tablespoons honey

3 tablespoons Sriracha

1 tablespoon lime juice

1. Preheat griddle to medium high.
2. Melt butter in a small saucepan on medium low heat; when melted add ginger and garlic. Stir until fragrant, about 2 minutes.
3. Fold in smoked paprika, ground cloves, honey, Sriracha and lime juice. Stir to combine, turn heat to medium and simmer for 5 minutes.
4. Rinse and pat chicken thighs dry.
5. Season with salt and pepper on both sides.
6. Spray griddle with non-stick cooking spray.
7. Place chicken thighs on grill, skin side down first. Grill for 5 minutes. Flip the chicken over and grill on the other side for 5 minutes.
8. Continue to cook chicken, flipping every 3 minutes, so it doesn't burn, until the internal temperature reads 165°F on a meat thermometer.
9. During the last 5 minutes of grilling brush the glaze on both sides of the chicken.
10. Remove from grill and serve warm.

Nutrition

Calories: 375, Sodium: 221mg, Dietary Fiber: 0.3g, Fat: 22.5g, Carbs: 14.7g, Protein: 32g

6

Main Dishes:
Beef

Caprese
Flank Steak

A super-fresh take on steak, this recipe elevates the delicious flank cut of steak to a whole new level. Best served with grilled eggplant, salad, pasta and a glass of Sangiovese for one decadent, Italian-inspired meal.

Servings: 4
Prep time: 10 minutes
Cook time: 10 minutes

4 (6 ounce) flank steaks
Sea salt, for seasoning
Flakey sea salt, for serving
Fresh ground pepper
Olive oil, premium brand
2 roma tomatoes, sliced
4 ounces fresh buffalo
   mozzarella, cut into four
   slices
8 fresh basil leaves
Balsamic vinegar glaze, for
   drizzling

1. Lightly brush each filet, on all sides, with olive oil and season with salt and pepper.

2. Preheat grill to high. Place steaks on grill, reduce heat to medium, tent with foil and cook for 5 minutes.

3. Flip, re-tent, and cook for an additional 5 minutes; during the last 2 minutes of grilling top each with a slice of mozzarella.

4. Remove steaks from the grill and top each with a few tomato slices, 2 basil leafs.

5. Drizzle with balsamic glaze, and sprinkle with flakey salt and a little more black pepper.

Nutrition

Calories: 461, Sodium:485mg, Dietary Fiber: 0.8g, Fat: 22.8g, Carbs: 5.7g, Protein: 55.9g

Coffee-Rubbed
Texas-Style Brisket

Coffee makes for a decadent rub when it comes to seasoning juicy steak to perfection. Slow cooked on low heat all day, you'll love making this for your next backyard barbecue or family fun day at home.

Servings: 6
Prep time: 10 minutes
Cook time: 6 hrs 20 minutes

1 (4 1/2 lb) flat cut beef brisket (about 3 inches thick)

For the rub:

1 tablespoon ground coffee

1 tablespoon sea salt

1 tablespoon dark brown sugar

2 teaspoons smoked paprika

2 teaspoons chili powder

1 teaspoon garlic powder

1 teaspoon onion powder

1 teaspoon ground black pepper

1 teaspoon mesquite liquid smoke, like Colgin

1. Combine the rub ingredients in a small mixing bowl.
2. Rinse and pat brisket dry and rub with coffee mix.
3. Preheat the grill for indirect grilling; heat one side to high and leaving one side with low heat.
4. Sear on high heat side for 3 - 5 minutes on each side or until nicely charred.
5. Move to low heat side, tent with foil, and cook for 6 hours or until a meat thermometer registers 195°.
6. Remove from grill. Let stand, covered, 30 minutes.
7. Cut brisket across grain into thin slices and serve.

Nutrition

Calories:591, Sodium: 3953mg, Dietary Fiber: 0.7g, Fat: 42.8g, Carbs: 3.2g, Protein: 45.9g

Tender Steak
with Pineapple Rice

Sticky, sweet pineapple rice is one delicious compliment to tender grilled steak. You'll definitely impress family and friends with this yummy recipe when you serve it with grilled veggies and iced green tea.

Servings: 4
Prep time: 10 minutes
Cook time: 10 minutes

4 (4-ounce) beef fillets

¼ cup soy sauce

½ teaspoon black pepper

½ teaspoon garlic powder

1 (8-ounce) can pineapple chunks, in juice, drained

2 scallions, thin sliced

2 (8.8-ounce) packages pre-cooked brown rice, like Uncle Ben's

7/8 teaspoon kosher salt

Olive oil, for brushing

1. Combine soy sauce, pepper, garlic powder, and beef in a large sealable plastic bag.

2. Seal and massage sauce into beef; let stand at room temperature for 7 minutes, turning bag occasionally.

3. Preheat griddle to medium-high heat and brush with olive oil.

4. Add pineapple and green onions to grill and cook 5 minutes or until well charred, turning to char evenly.

5. Remove pineapple mix and brush with additional olive oil.

6. Add steaks and cook 3 minutes on each side, for rare, or until desired temperature is reached.

7. Cook rice according to package instructions.

8. Add rice, pineapple, onions, and salt to a bowl and stir gently to combine.

9. Plate steaks with pineapple rice and serve!

Nutrition

Calories: 369, Sodium: 1408mg, Dietary Fiber: 2.1g, Fat: 12.4g, Carbs: 37g, Protein: 27.9g

Mexican Grilled
Steak Salad

Juicy steak is the perfect way to top a Mexican-inspired salad. Spice meets creamy avocado dressing for a healthy way to enjoy steak for both lunch and dinner!

Servings: 2
Prep time: 10 minutes
Cook time: 10 minutes

1. Make marinade, then marinate steak for 4 hours to overnight.
2. Combine salad ingredients in a large bowl; add dressing and mix well. Place salad on separate plates.
3. Preheat grill to high. Place marinated steak on grill, reduce heat to medium, tent with foil and cook for 5 minutes.
4. Flip, re-tent, and cook for an additional 5 minutes.
5. Remove steak from the grill and slice into 2 inch strips.
6. Place steak strips on individual salads, and sprinkle with flakey salt and a little black pepper. Garnish with cilantro.

Steak marinade:

2 tablespoons olive oil
3 garlic cloves, minced
2 teaspoons chili powder
1 teaspoon ground cumin
1 teaspoon kosher salt
1 teaspoon freshly ground pepper
1 1/2 pounds skirt or flap steak, cut into 4-inch lengths
½ cup lager beer

Salad:

12 ounces romaine hearts, trimmed and chopped
1 can black beans, drained and rinsed
1 pint cherry tomatoes, halved
1 large ripe avocado, pitted, peeled, and cut into chunks
About 1/3 cup crumbled queso fresco
Chopped fresh cilantro, for garnish
Kosher salt

Dressing:

1 large ripe avocado, pitted, peeled, and cut into chunks
½ cup plain, whole-milk Greek yogurt
1/3 cup chopped fresh cilantro
Zest of 1 lime
Juice of 2 limes

Nutrition

Calories: 1332, Sodium: 2011mg, Dietary Fiber: 13.3g, Fat: 65.1g, Carbs:29.4g, Protein: 152.3g

Rib-Eye Steak
with Herbed Steak Butter

Grilled rib-eye is one tender, delicious way to enjoy steak - especially topped with creamy, herbed French butter. Decadent meets succulent in this grilling combination of perfectly blended flavors. Serve with mashed potatoes and the grilled asparagus recipe below for one delicious meal.

Servings: 2 - 4
Prep time: 12 hours
Cook time: 50 minutes

1 (24-ounce) bone-in Tomahawk rib-eye, about 2 1/2 inches thick

Olive oil

Sea salt

Fresh cracked pepper

3 tablespoons premium French butter

½ teaspoon Herbes de Provence

1. Beat butter with herbs in a small mixing bowl, cover and refrigerate until ready to grill rib-eye.

2. Rub the rib-eye liberally with olive oil, salt and pepper until entire steak is covered.

3. Wrap lightly with cling wrap and place in the refrigerator to marinate for 12 hours.

4. Preheat the griddle to high heat on one side and medium low on the other side, at least one hour prior to cooking.

5. Remove the steak from the refrigerator and leave at room temperature during the hour that the grill is preheating.

6. Place the steak on the center of the hottest side of the grill and rotate left and right to get proper grill marks. Do this for both sides, about 10 minutes.

7. Move the rib-eye to the cooler side of the grill and cook to rare, about 25 to 30 minutes.

8. Transfer rib-eye to a grill rack, add herbed butter on top, and lightly tent it with tin foil to rest for at least 15 minutes before carving.

9. Serve with your favorite sides!

Nutrition

Calories: 549, Sodium: 607mg, Dietary Fiber: 1.5g, Fat: 40.3g, Carbs: 3.5g, Protein: 40.9g

High-Low
Strip Steak

High-low strip steaks are the perfect way to quickly grill up a delicious NY Strip steak. Scrumptiously seasoned, these steaks pair deliciously with creamy mashed potatoes and grilled asparagus.

Servings: 2
Prep time: 8 -12 hours
Cook time: 15 minutes

2 (1-pound) New York strip steaks, trimmed

For the rub:

1 bunch thyme sprigs
1 bunch rosemary sprigs
1 bunch sage sprigs
1 1/2 teaspoons black pepper, divided
3/4 teaspoon sea salt, divided
1/2 teaspoon garlic powder
2 tablespoons chopped fresh flat-leaf parsley
2 tablespoons extra-virgin olive oil

For the basting liquid:

1/4 cup extra-virgin olive oil
1 tablespoon onion powder
1 tablespoon chopped fresh thyme
1 tablespoon sugar
1 teaspoon butter, unsalted
1 teaspoon Worcestershire sauce
1/2 teaspoon freshly ground black pepper
1/4 teaspoon kosher salt
1/4 teaspoon crushed red pepper

1. Combine basting liquid ingredients in a saucepan and bring to a simmer over medium heat. Remove from heat; refrigerate in an airtight container overnight.

2. Preheat griddle to high heat.

3. Combine rub ingredients in a small mixing bowl and rub steaks with spice mixture; let rest 10 minutes.

4. Combine basting liquid ingredients in a small mixing bowl; reserve half for serving.

5. Place steaks on grill and cook 1 minute per side; baste with basting liquid frequently.

6. Turn griddle down to medium heat.

7. Turn steaks and grill 3 additional minutes per side; or until thermometer registers 135°F for medium rare.

8. Remove steaks to a platter; baste with basting liquid using herb brush. Let stand 15 minutes.

9. Let rest 5 minutes. Cut steaks across grain into thin slices.

10. Serve steaks with reserved basting liquid.

Nutrition

Calories:755, Sodium: 1374mg, Dietary Fiber: 2.5g, Fat: 32.4g, Carbs:13.7g, Protein: 102.7g

Greek Flank Steak
Gyros

Grilled flank steak makes for the perfect protein to stuff inside warmed pita pockets. When you're craving a taste of Greece be sure to serve this alongside hummus and carrots with a glass of sparkling water and lemon.

Servings: 4
Prep Time: 5 minutes
Cook Time: 20 minutes

1 pound flank steak
1 white onion, thinly sliced
1 roma tomato, thinly sliced
1 cucumber, peeled and thinly sliced
1/4 cup crumbled feta cheese
4 6-inch pita pockets

For the marinade:

1/4 cup olive oil, plus more for brushing
1 teaspoon dried oregano
1 teaspoon balsamic vinegar
1 teaspoon garlic powder
Sea salt and freshly ground pepper, to taste

For the sauce:

1 cup plain yogurt
2 tablespoons fresh dill (can use dried), chopped
1 teaspoon garlic, minced
2 tablespoons lemon juice

1. Cut the flank steak into thin strips against the grain. Add the marinade ingredients to a large sealable plastic bag, add the sliced meat, seal, and turn to coat.

2. Place in the refrigerator to marinate for 2 hours or overnight.

3. Preheat the griddle to medium-high heat, and an oven to 250°F.

4. Combine the sauce ingredients in small mixing bowl and set aside.

5. Spritz the pitas with a little water, wrap in foil and place in the oven to warm.

6. Brush griddle with olive oil.

7. Add meat to grill and discard marinade. Cook until brown and cooked through, about 5 minutes.

8. Remove the pitas from the oven, and cut in half.

9. Arrange the pitas on plates and stuff with cucumber, tomato, onions, and beef.

10. Spoon some yogurt sauce over the meat and top with feta and serve.

Nutrition

Calories:901, Sodium: 1221mg, Dietary Fiber: 5.7g, Fat: 27.2g, Carbs:107.8g, Protein: 53.5g

Coffee & Brown Sugar-Crusted
Skirt Steak with Grilled Okra and Jalapeños

Serve up something delicious for dinner when you grill up skirt steak with okra and jalapenos. You'll love this recipe served with a side of brown rice and a glass of Malbec or sparkling water.

Servings: 8
Prep time: 10 minutes
Cook time: 20 minutes

1/4 cup espresso, finely ground

1/4 cup dark brown sugar, firmly packed

1 1/2 teaspoon sea salt

1/8 teaspoon ground cinnamon

1/8 teaspoon ground ginger

1/8 teaspoon ground white pepper

1/8 teaspoon five-spice powder

Pinch cayenne pepper

2 1/2 lb. skirt steak, cut into 4 pieces

1 tablespoon olive oil

2 cups fresh okra, whole

2 cups jalapenos, whole

1. Heat grill to high.

2. Combine coffee, brown sugar, salt, cinnamon, ginger, white pepper, five-spice powder, and cayenne pepper in a bowl to make rub.

3. Remove steak from refrigerator and let come to room temperature, about 15 minutes. Rub steak with oil, and sprinkle with spice rub. Massage spice rub into meat.

4. Grill until charred and medium-rare, 2 to 4 minutes per side. Transfer to a cutting board, cover with foil and let rest 5 minutes before thinly slicing at an angle.

5. While steak is covered and resting, grill okra and jalapenos for 5 minutes on high heat. When slightly charred, sprinkle with salt and serve immediately with steak.

Nutrition

Calories:324, Sodium: 461mg, Dietary Fiber: 0.1g, Fat: 16g, Carbs: 4.6g, Protein: 37.9g

Tuscan-Style Steak
with Crispy Potatoes

Sweet and savory, this recipes calls for an Italian twist on classic meat and potatoes you'll absolutely love.

Servings: 4
Prep time: 30 minutes
Cook time: 35 minutes

2 bone-in porterhouse steaks

1 1/2 lb. small potatoes, like Yukon Gold, scrubbed but skins left on, halved

4 tablespoons extra-virgin olive oil, divided

Sea salt and freshly ground pepper, to taste

2 teaspoons red wine, like Sangiovese or Montepulciano

1 teaspoon balsamic vinegar

pinch red pepper flakes

3 fresh rosemary sprigs, needles removed (discard stems)

1. Add potatoes to a large pot and cover with water, bring to a boil over high heat, then reduce the heat to medium-high and cook until the potatoes are almost tender, about 10 minutes. Drain, add to a medium mixing bowl, coat with 2 tablespoons olive oil, and set aside.

2. Preheat grill to medium heat.

3. Whisk 2 tablespoons olive oil, rosemary needles, red wine, vinegar, and pepper flakes; add steaks to marinade and set aside until ready to grill.

4. Sprinkle potatoes with salt and pepper.

5. Add steaks to one side of the grill and potatoes to the other.

6. Cook steak for 5 minutes, flip and 4 minutes on the other side for medium rare.

7. Add the potatoes to cook for 5 minutes.

8. Transfer steaks to a cutting board and tent with aluminum foil and let rest for 5 minutes while potatoes are cooking.

9. Divide each steak into 2 pieces and divide among 4 dinner plates. Spoon some potatoes around the steak and serve hot!

Nutrition

Calories:366, Sodium: 153mg, Dietary Fiber: 4.5g, Fat: 23.3g, Carbs: 27.3g, Protein: 13.4g

NY Strip Steaks
with Sweet-Spicy Hoisin Sauce

Sweet and spicy hoisin sauce is the perfect complement to a delicious NY strip steak. Serve this delicious steak with brown rice, your favorite flash grilled veggies, and iced green tea for a delicious, quick Asian-inspired meal.

Servings: 6
Prep time: 15 minutes
Cook time: 35 minutes

6 (8 ounce) NY strip steaks

2 large sweet onions, sliced crosswise 1/2 inch thick

Sea salt and fresh ground black pepper

1/4 cup olive oil, plus more for rubbing

4 medium shallots, thinly sliced

4 garlic cloves, minced

1 tablespoon finely grated ginger

1/2 teaspoon crushed red pepper

1/3 cup chopped cilantro

1/3 cup hoisin sauce

3 tablespoons soy sauce

1/2 cup chicken stock

3 tablespoons honey

3 tablespoons unsalted butter

1. Preheat griddle to medium-high.

2. Heat the oil, shallots, garlic, ginger, crushed red pepper and cilantro in a saucepan over medium heat, stirring occasionally, until softened, about 7 minutes.

3. Add the hoisin, soy sauce and chicken stock, raise the heat to medium-high and boil until thickened, about 5 minutes.

4. Fold in the honey.

5. Remove from heat and stir in the butter until well-blended; keep warm.

6. Generously rub the steaks and onions with olive oil and season with salt and pepper.

7. Grill the steaks for 4 minutes per side.

8. Transfer the steaks to a carving board and let rest for 5 minutes.

9. Grill the onions for 4 minutes per side, or until charred. Transfer the onions to a plate.

10. Serve steaks with onions, hoisin sauce, and your favorite sides.

Nutrition

Calories: 703, Sodium: 3536mg, Dietary Fiber: 1.8g, Fat: 38.9g, Carbs: 22.8g, Protein: 63.5g

Greek Feta & Spinach
Burgers

Turn your favorite burgers into a Greek feast with these decadently stuffed burgers. You'll love this served with turnip fries and hummus!

Servings: 2
Prep time: 25 minutes
Cook time: 8 minutes

1/2 pound lean ground beef

2 tablespoons crumbled reduced-fat feta cheese

1 clove garlic, minced

1/8 teaspoon ground black pepper

1 whole wheat hamburger bun, split and toasted

2 teaspoons tzatziki, for garnish

1/2 cup fresh spinach leaves, for garnish

2 tomato slices, for garnish

Sliced red onion, for garnish

1. In a medium bowl combine ground beef, feta cheese, garlic, and pepper. Shape mixture into two 1/2-inch-thick patties.

2. Preheat griddle to medium-high heat and cook for 4 minutes, flip, and cook 4 more minutes; or until an instant-read thermometer inserted patties reads 160°F.

3. Spread tzatziki on each bun top. Line bun with spinach. Top bottom bun with burgers.

4. Top burger with tomato slices, red onion, then the spinach lined bun top and serve.

Nutrition

Calories: 377, Sodium: 493mg, Dietary Fiber: 3.2g, Fat: 12.8g, Carbs:17.7g, Protein: 42.3g

Basic Juicy
NY Strip Steak

When you are craving a basic, juicy steak with no frills - this is the recipe to try our on you Blackstone Outdoor Griddle Station. Simple and succulent, this steak is for those who love bare bones seasoning without sacrificing flavor.

Servings 1
Prep time: 45 minutes
Cook time: 8 minutes

1 (8 ounce) NY strip steak
Olive oil
Sea salt
Fresh ground black pepper

1. Remove the steak from the refrigerator and let it come to room temperature, about 30 to 45 minutes.

2. Preheat griddle to medium-high heat and brush with olive oil.

3. Season the steak on all sides with salt and pepper.

4. Cook steak about 4 to 5 minutes.

5. Flip and cook about 4 minutes more for medium rare steak; between 125°F and 130°F on a meat thermometer.

6. Transfer the steak to a plate and let it rest for 5 minutes before serving.

Nutrition

Calories:1560, Sodium: 8468mg, Dietary Fiber: 0.g, Fat: 86g, Carbs: 0.1g, Protein: 184g

Caprese Grilled
Filet Mignon

Serve up something healthy, with these tender fillets topped with a taste of the Mediterranean. Serve with creamy risotto, succulent grilled scallops and your favorite red wine for a surf and turf dream meal right at home.

Servings: 4
Prep time: 10 minutes
Cook time: 10 minutes

4 (6 ounce) filets

1 teaspoon garlic salt

Italian Olive oil

2 roma tomatoes, sliced

4 ounces fresh buffalo mozzarella, cut into four slices

8 fresh basil leaves

Balsamic vinegar glaze, for drizzling

Sea salt, for seasoning

Fresh ground pepper

1. Lightly brush each filet, on all sides, with olive oil and rub with garlic salt.

2. Preheat grill to high. Place steaks on grill, reduce heat to medium, tent with foil and cook for 5 minutes.

3. Flip, re-tent, and cook for an additional 5 minutes; during the last 2 minutes of grilling top each with a slice of mozzarella.

4. Remove steaks from the grill and top each with a few tomato slices, 2 basil leafs.

5. Drizzle with balsamic, sprinkle with sea salt and black pepper and serve.

Nutrition

Calories: 406, Sodium: 688mg, Dietary Fiber: 0.8g, Fat: 21.8g, Carbs: 7.2g, Protein: 45.1g

Flank Steak
with Garlic and Rosemary

Flavorful and delicious, the flank steak is perfect complimented with robust garlic and spicy rosemary. Serve on top of a bed or your favorite greens dressed with balsamic vinegar and olive oil for one very healthy meal.

Servings: 4
Prep time: 10 minutes
Cook time: 20 minutes

2 (8 ounce) flank steaks

For the marinade:

1 tablespoon extra virgin olive oil, plus more for brushing

2 tablespoons fresh rosemary, chopped

4 cloves garlic, minced

2 teaspoons sea salt

1/4 teaspoon black pepper

1. Add marinade ingredients to a food processor or blender and pulse until garlic and rosemary are pulverized.

2. Use a fork to pierce the steaks 10 times on each side.

3. Rub each evenly with the marinade on both sides.

4. Place in a covered dish and refrigerate for at least 1 hour or overnight.

5. Preheat grill to high and brush with olive oil and preheat to high.

6. Cook steaks for 5 minutes, flip, tent with foil, and cook for about 3-4 minutes more.

7. Transfer meat to rest on a cutting board, cover with aluminum foil, for about 15 minutes.

8. Slice very thin against the grain and serve immediately.

Nutrition

Calories: 260, Sodium: 1001mg, Dietary Fiber: 0.8g, Fat: 13.2g, Carbs: 2.1g, Protein: 31.8g

Beef Pinwheels

Beef Pinwheels are a delicious way to serve up something different. Great for dinner parties, this appetizer can be served on a bed of arugula tossed in lemon juice or all on it's very own.

Servings: 4 - 8
Prep time: 10 minutes
Cook time: 8 minutes

1 pound Sirloin, cut into
   4 1/2-inch thick pieces
1 tablespoon salt
olive oil, for rubbing pinwheels
freshly ground pepper

For the stuffing:

1 jar red pesto
2 tablespoons pancetta
1 clove garlic

1. Preheat griddle to medium-high heat.
2. Pre-soak a dozen toothpicks in warm water.
3. Add stuffing ingredients to a food processor or blender and pulse until well-combined.
4. Pound out the sirloin pieces until super-thin.
5. Season the sirloin pieces generously with oil, salt and pepper.
6. Spoon stuffing on top of each of the pieces.
7. Roll up like a jelly roll and secure on either end with soaked toothpicks.
8. Grill the pinwheels for 3 to 4 minutes per side, rotating to evenly cook.
9. Allow to rest for 5 minutes and serve.

Nutrition

Calories: 363, Sodium: 1643mg, Dietary Fiber: 1.7g, Fat: 25.3g, Carbs: 1.7g, Protein: 29.6g

Carne Asada
Perfection

Grill up a taste of Mexico with this delicious Carne Asada recipe. Charred steak, seasoned to perfection can be served as a main dish or as the ingredient in several of your favorite Mexican inspired meals like tacos and burritos.

Servings: 4
Prep time: 1 - 2 hours
Cook time: 15 minutes

1 lb. arrachera or hanger steak, sliced thin

1/4 cup olive oil

1 lime, juiced

1 orange, juiced

1 garlic clove, finely chopped

1/2 teaspoon cumin

1/4 teaspoon salt

1/4 teaspoon ground pepper

handful of fresh cilantro, chopped

1. Combine all of the ingredients in a large sealable plastic bag. Marinate in the refrigerator for 1 to 2 hours.

2. Preheat to medium/high heat, grill for 2 minutes on each side or until just cooked through.

3. Transfer to cutting board to rest for 10 minutes.

4. Slice against the grain and serve.

Nutrition

Calories: 363, Sodium: 200mg, Dietary Fiber: 1.7g, Fat: 18.4g, Carbs: 7.7g, Protein: 41.6g

Rib Eye Steak
with Romaine Marmalade and Watercress

Crispy romaine meats tangy watercress and citrus sweet notes for an elevated way to serve a rib-eye. Easy to make, the whole family will love this bright steak served with iced tea or a crisp lager.

Servings: 6
Prep time: 10 minutes
Cook time: 40 minutes

Steak:

One 24-ounce bone-in rib eye chop, about 2 1/2 inches thick
Extra virgin olive oil
Flaky sea salt
Cracked pepper

Romaine Marmalade and Watercress:

4 bunches organic watercress, stems removed
2 whole leaves romaine lettuce, chopped
1 small clove garlic, minced
1/4 bunch fresh cilantro, trimmed and chopped fine
1/4 bunch fresh flat-leaf parsley, trimmed and chopped fine
1 lemon, juiced
1 teaspoon orange marmalade
Flakey sea salt, to taste
Fresh ground pepper, to taste
2 tablespoons extra-virgin olive oil

1. Rub the rib-eye liberally with olive oil, salt and pepper until entire steak is covered.
2. Wrap lightly with cling wrap and place in the refrigerator to marinate for 12 hours.
3. Preheat the griddle to high heat on one side and medium low on the other side, at least one hour prior to cooking.
4. Remove the steak from the refrigerator and leave at room temperature during the hour that the grill is preheating.
5. Combine romaine marmalade and watercress ingredients in a large mixing bowl and set aside.
6. Place the steak on the center of the hottest side of the grill and rotate left and right to get proper grill marks. Do this for both sides, about 10 minutes.
7. Move the rib-eye to the cooler side of the grill and cook to rare, about 25 to 30 minutes.
8. Transfer rib-eye to a grill rack, add romaine marmalade on top, and lightly tent it with tin foil to rest for at least 15 minutes before carving.
9. Serve with your favorite sides!

Nutrition

Calories: 293, Sodium: 271mg, Dietary Fiber: 1.1g, Fat: 8.6g, Carbs: 9g, Protein: 42.8g

Flash-Marinated
Skirt Steak

Flash marinated flank steak is the perfect steak when your pressed for time. Quick and easy to marinate, don't be afraid to prepare the recipe in the morning and cook it right after work!

Servings: 4
Prep time: 30 minutes
Cook time: 45 minutes

2 (8 ounce) skirt steaks

For the marinade:

2 tablespoons balsamic vinegar

2 teaspoons olive oil, more for brushing

2 garlic cloves, minced

Sea salt, to taste

Black pepper, to taste

1. Combine marinade ingredients in a sealable plastic bag, add steaks, seal bag, turn to coat; let stand at room temperature for 30 minutes.

2. Preheat griddle to medium-high heat.

3. Remove steaks and discard marinade, place on griddle and cook about 3 minutes per side. Transfer steaks to cutting board and rest for 5 Minutes.

4. Cut across the grain into slices and serve with your favorite sides.

Nutrition

Calories: 256, Sodium: 204mg, Dietary Fiber: 0g, Fat: 13.8g, Carbs: 0.6g, Protein: 30.3g

7

Main Dishes:
Pork

Sticky-Sweet
Pork Shoulder

Sweet and sticky sauce is the perfect complement to savory grilled pork. Serve this delicious dish with your favorite sides or as a delicious stuffing for steamed buns or grilled bread.

Servings: 6 - 8
Prep time: 8 hours
Cook time: 8 minutes

1 (5 lbs.) Boston Butt pork shoulder

For the marinade:

2 tablespoons garlic, minced
1 large piece ginger, peeled and chopped
1 cup hoisin sauce
3/4 cup fish sauce
2/3 cup honey
2/3 cup Shaoxing
1/2 cup chili oil
1/3 cup oyster sauce
1/3 cup sesame oil

For the glaze:

¾ cup dark brown sugar
1 tablespoon light molasses

1. Place pork shoulder, fat side down, on a cutting board with a short end facing you. Holding a long sharp knife about 1"–1½" above cutting board, make a shallow cut along the entire length of a long side of shoulder.

2. Continue cutting deeper into meat, lifting and unfurling with your free hand, until it lies flat.

3. Purée marinade in a blender and reserve 1 ½ cups for glaze, cover and refrigerate.

4. Pour remaining marinade in a large sealable plastic bag.

5. Add pork shoulder to bag and marinate in the refrigerator for 8 hours.

6. Preheat griddle to medium heat (with cover closed, thermometer should register 350°). Remove pork from marinade, letting excess drip off.

7. Add glaze ingredients to reserved marinade until sugar is dissolved.

8. Grill pork, for 8 minutes, basting and turning with tongs every minute or so, until thick coated with glaze, lightly charred in spots, and warmed through; an instant-read thermometer inserted into the thickest part should register 145°F.

9. Transfer to a cutting board and slice against the grain, ¼" thick, to serve.

Nutrition

Calories: 1286, Sodium: 2875mg, Dietary Fiber: 1g, Fat: 84.8g, Carbs: 58.3g, Protein: 68.7g

A Quick-Start™ Cookbook: COOKING WITH THE BLACKSTONE OUTDOOR GAS GRIDDLE

Pineapple Bacon
Pork Chops

Sweet and juicy pineapple compliments savory pork for one incredible dish! You'll love the sweet and spicy kick in this recipe - serve it with your favorite grilled side dishes and vegetables and a cold glass of beer or iced tea.

Servings: 6
Prep time: 30 minutes
Cook time: 1 hour

1 large whole pineapple
6 pork chops
12 slices thick-cut bacon
12 toothpicks, soaked in water
for 1 hour

For the glaze:
¼ cup honey
1/8 teaspoon cayenne pepper

1. Turn both burners to medium-high heat; after about 15 minutes, turn off one of the middle burners and turn the remaining burners down to medium.

2. Slice off the top and bottom of the pineapple, and peel the pineapple, cutting the skin off in strips.

3. Cut pineapple flesh into six quarters.

4. Wrap each pineapple section with a bacon slice; secure each end with a toothpick.

5. Brush quarters with honey and sprinkle with cayenne pepper.

6. Put the quarters on the griddle, flipping when bacon is cooked so that both sides are evenly grilled.

7. While pineapple quarters are cooking, coat pork chops with honey and cayenne pepper. Set on grill.

8. Tent with foil and cook for 20 minutes. Flip, and continue cooking an additional 10 to 20 minutes or until chops are fully cooked.

9. Serve each chop with a pineapple quarter on the side.

Nutrition
Calories: 380 Sodium: 852mg, Dietary Fiber: 0.5g, Fat: 23.5g, Carbs: 18.2g, Protein: 25.8g

Moroccan Spiced
Pork Tenderloin with Creamy Harissa Sauce

Moroccan spice and creamy harissa make for one delicious way to serve up tender pork any night of the week. Enjoy this yummy dish with collard greens and potato salad for a taste twist on your next cookout.

Servings: 6
Prep: 40 minutes
Cook: 20 minutes

2 (1 lb.) pork tenderloins
1 teaspoon ground cinnamon
1 teaspoon ground cilantro
1 teaspoon ground cumin
1 teaspoon paprika
1 teaspoon sea salt
2 tablespoons olive oil

For Creamy Harissa Sauce:

1 cup Greek yogurt (8 ounces)
1 tablespoon fresh lemon juice
1 tablespoon extra-virgin olive oil
1 teaspoon harissa sauce
1 clove garlic, minced
Kosher salt and cracked black pepper

1. Combine harissa ingredients in a small mixing bowl and set aside.
2. Combine the cinnamon, coriander, cumin, paprika, salt and olive oil.
3. Rub the seasonings evenly over the pork tenderloins; cover and refrigerate for 30 minutes.
4. Preheat griddle to high-heat and cook tenderloins until browned; about 8 to 10 minutes.
5. Turn and cook an additional 8 to 10 minutes. Transfer the tenderloins to a cutting board, tent with foil and rest for 10 minutes.
6. Slice and serve with creamy harissa sauce.

Nutrition

Calories: 376, Sodium: 458mg, Dietary Fiber: 0.4g, Fat: 17.9g, Carbs: 2.6g, Protein: 48.7g

Big John's
Chili-Rubbed Ribs

Take your ribs to a whole new level with chili rub that is lip smacking good. If you love dry rubbed, juicy ribs this is the recipe to whip up!

Servings: 10
Prep time: 30 minutes
Cook time: 1 hr 30 minutes

6 pounds baby back pork ribs

For the rub:

3 tablespoons brown sugar
2 tablespoons smoked paprika
2 tablespoons chili powder
3 teaspoons ground cumin
2 teaspoons garlic powder
1 teaspoon salt

For the glaze:

1 cup reduced-sodium soy
   sauce
1 cup packed brown sugar
2/3 cup ketchup
1/3 cup lemon juice
1-1/2 teaspoons minced fresh
   ginger root
½ teaspoon red pepper flakes

1. Mix the rub ingredients and rub over ribs. Refrigerate, covered, for 30 minutes.
2. Wrap rib racks in aluminum foil and seal tightly.
3. Grill over indirect medium heat 1 to 1-1/2 hours or until tender.
4. Combine glaze ingredients in a saucepan and cook, uncovered, over medium heat for 8 minutes or until heated through and sugar is dissolved, stirring occasionally.
5. Remove ribs from foil.
6. Place ribs over direct heat; brush with the glaze.
7. Grill, covered, over medium heat 25 to 30 additional minutes or until browned, turning and brushing ribs occasionally with remaining glaze.
8. Serve hot!

Nutrition

Calories: 439, Sodium: 1382mg, Dietary Fiber: 1,5g, Fat: 33.1g, Carbs:11.4g, Protein: 23.9g

Habanero–Marinated
Pork Chops

Kick things up a notch on your Blackstone Outdoor Griddle Station with this spicy recipe. These yummy pork chops pair perfectly with yellow rice, black beans, and your favorite salad.

Servings: 4
Prep time: 30 minutes
Cook time: 13 minutes

4 ½-inch-thick bone-in pork chops

3 tablespoons olive oil, plus more for grill

Kosher salt and freshly ground black pepper

For the marinade:

1 habanero chile, seeded, chopped fine

2 garlic cloves, minced

½ cup fresh orange juice

2 tablespoons brown sugar

1 tablespoon apple cider vinegar

1. Combine marinade ingredients in a large sealable plastic bag.
2. Pierce pork chops all over with a fork and add to bag, seal, and turn to coat.
3. Marinate at room temperature, turning occasionally, for 30 minutes.
4. Prepare grill for medium-high heat.
5. Brush with oil.
6. Remove pork chops from marinade and pat dry.
7. Grill for 8 minutes, turning occasionally, until charred and cooked through.
8. Transfer to a plate and let rest 5 minutes.
9. Serve with your favorite sides.

Nutrition

Calories: 490 Sodium: 171mg, Dietary Fiber: 1.1g, Fat: 39.2g, Carbs: 10.9g, Protein: 23.3g

Sweet & Spicy
BBQ Ribs

Sweet and spicy ribs are a great way to grill out with the whole family on the weekends. Serve these sticky ribs with mashed potatoes and grilled vegetables for some decadent weekend backyard fun.

Servings: 4 - 6
Prep time: 8 hours
Cook time: 1 hour

2 Racks St Louis Style Ribs

2 bottles BBQ sauce, like Stubbs or Kraft

For the Rub:

2 tablespoon paprika

1 1/2 tablespoon dark brown sugar

1 tablespoon garlic powder

1 tablespoon chili powder

1 tablespoon sea salt

1 1/2 teaspoon onion powder

1 1/2 teaspoon black pepper

½ teaspoon red chili flakes

1. Combine rub ingredients in a small mixing bowl; rub evenly over the ribs. Marinate overnight in refrigerator.

2. Preheat the oven to 300°F. Place the ribs on a foil lined sheet pan, cover with foil and bake for an hour.

3. Baste the ribs, and continue to baste every 30-45 minutes; cook an additional 2 hours.

4. Remove the ribs from the oven, and baste them with more sauce.

5. Preheat griddle to medium high.

6. Transfer ribs to grill and cook 10 minutes, basting regularly with the BBQ sauce.

7. Take them off grill, cover with foil, and let rest for 30 minutes.

8. Serve with your favorite sides.

Nutrition

Calories: 349 Sodium: 2112mg, Dietary Fiber: 2.4g, Fat: 13.1g, Carbs: 47.2g, Protein: 11.5g

Herb-Crusted
Mediterranean Pork Tenderloin

Herb-Crusted Tenderloin with Mediterranean style spices is one great way to grill up juicy tenderloin. My favorite way to serve this dish is alongside lemon chili pasta and salad with a glass of Pinot Grigio.

Servings: 4
Prep time: 2 hours
Cook time: 30 minutes

1 pound pork tenderloin
1 tablespoon olive oil
2 teaspoons dried oregano
3/4 teaspoon lemon pepper
1 teaspoon garlic powder
¼ cup parmesan cheese, grated
3 tablespoons olive tapenade

1. Place pork on a large piece of plastic wrap.
2. Rub tenderloin with oil, and sprinkle oregano, garlic powder, and lemon pepper evenly over entire tenderloin.
3. Wrap tightly in the plastic wrap and refrigerate for 2 hours.
4. Preheat griddle to medium-high heat.
5. Transfer pork to cutting board, remove plastic wrap, and make a lengthwise cut through center of tenderloin, opening meat so it lies flat, but do not cut all the way through.
6. Combine tapenade and parmesan in a small mixing bowl; rub into the center of the tenderloin and fold meat back together.
7. Tie together with twine in 2-inch intervals.
8. Grill tenderloin for 20 minutes, turning tenderloin once during grilling, or until internal temperature reaches 145°F.
9. Transfer tenderloin to cutting board.
10. Tent with foil; let rest for 10 minutes.
11. Remove string and cut into 1/4-inch-thick slices and serve.

Nutrition

Calories: 413 Sodium: 1279mg, Dietary Fiber: 0.5g, Fat: 30.5g, Carbs: 2.4g, Protein: 31.4g

Dijon Honey
Pork Chops with Tomato-Peach Salad

Transform your weeknight dinners with this delicious grilled pork chop recipe. Tangy Dijon mustard makes the perfect seasoning for juicy pork when served with a sweet salad on the side.

Servings: 4
Prep time: 10 minutes
Cook time: 25 minutes

4 (8 ounce) bone-in pork chops

1/4 cups Dijon mustard

1/4 cup, plus 2 tablespoons red wine vinegar

2 tablespoons honey

8 tablespoons extra-virgin olive oil, divided

2 large heirloom tomatoes, cut into chunks

3 peaches, sliced

1/4 cup basil leaves, torn, plus more for garnish

Sea salt

Freshly ground black pepper

1. Preheat an oven to 375°F. Place pork chops in a shallow glass baking dish.

2. Whisk together mustard, red wine vinegar, honey, and 4 tablespoons olive oil in a small mixing bowl.

3. Pour mixture over pork, turning to coat, and let rest 10 minutes.

4. Place tomatoes, peaches, and basil in a large mixing bowl.

5. Whisk together remaining 2 tablespoons vinegar and 4 tablespoons olive oil. Drizzle mixture over tomato-peach mixture and toss, and season with salt and pepper.

6. Heat griddle to medium-high heat.

7. Remove pork chops from marinade and season with salt and pepper.

8. Grill 3 minutes per side, then transfer pan to oven and finish cooking for 6 minutes; or until the internal temperature reads 145°.

9. Let rest 5 minutes, and serve with tomato-peach salad and garnish with torn basil.

Nutrition

Calories: 1126, Sodium: 564mg, Dietary Fiber: 2.8g, Fat: 90.8g, Carbs: 24.1g, Protein: 55.3g

Honey Soy
Pork Chops

Sweet and tangy grilled pork is absolutely delicious when grilled to perfection on your Blackstone Outdoor Griddle Station. Simply serve this dish with rice and grilled vegetables for one delicious meal.

Servings: 6
Prep time: 1 hour
Cook time: 25 minutes

6 (4 ounce) boneless pork chops
1/4 cup organic honey
1 to 2 tablespoons low sodium soy sauce
2 tablespoons olive oil
1 tablespoon rice mirin

1. Combine honey, soy sauce, oil, and white vinegar and whisk until well-combined. Add sauce and pork chops to a large sealable plastic bag and marinate for 1 hour.

2. Preheat the grill to medium-high heat and cook for 4 to 5 minutes, or until the pork chop easily releases from the grill.

3. Flip and continue to cook for 5 additional minutes, or until internal temperature reaches 145°F.

4. Serve and enjoy!

Nutrition

Calories: 251, Sodium: 187mg, Dietary Fiber: 0.1g, Fat: 8.7g, Carbs: 13.1g, Protein: 29.9g

Glazed
Country Ribs

Country ribs are full of delicious flavor and make for one great main dish on weeknights or weekends with friends. Serve these ribs with your favorite sides and cold, crisp beer on summer holidays for traditional grilling fun.

Servings: 6
Prep time: 10 minutes
Cook time: 4 hours

3 pounds country-style pork ribs

1 cup low-sugar ketchup

½ cup water

¼ cup onion, finely chopped

¼ cup cider vinegar or wine vinegar

¼ cup light molasses

2 tablespoons Worcestershire sauce

2 teaspoons chili powder

2 cloves garlic, minced

1. Combine ketchup, water, onion, vinegar, molasses, Worcestershire sauce, chili powder, and garlic in a saucepan and bring to boil; reduce heat. Simmer, uncovered, for 10 to 15 minutes or until desired thickness is reached, stirring often.

2. Trim fat from ribs.

3. Preheat grill to medium-high.

4. Place ribs, bone-side down, on grill and grill for 1-1/2 to 2 hours or until tender, brushing occasionally with sauce during the last 10 minutes of grilling.

5. Serve with remaining sauce and enjoy!

Nutrition

Calories: 404, Sodium: 733mg, Dietary Fiber: 0.4g, Fat: 8.1g, Carbs:15.2g, Protein: 60.4g

Pork Chops
with Herb Apple Compote

Apples are one of my absolute favorite ingredients to pair with pork chops, and I hope you love this recipe too! Sweet meets juicy pork for a grilling flavor that is out of this world.

Servings: 4
Prep time: 5 minutes
Cook time: 20 minutes

4, bone-in pork chops

2 honeycrisp apples, peeled, cored and chopped

1/3 cup orange juice

1 teaspoon chopped fresh rosemary

1 teaspoon chopped fresh sage

Sea salt

Black pepper

1. Add the apples, herbs and orange juice to a saucepan and simmer over medium heat until the apples are tender and the juices are thickened to a thin syrup, about 10 to 12 minutes.

2. Season pork chops with salt and pepper.

3. Place on the grill and cook until the pork chop releases from the grill, about 4 minutes.

4. Flip and cook on the other side for 3 minutes.

5. Transfer to a cutting board and tent with foil.

6. Top with apple compote and serve!

Nutrition

Calories: 284, Sodium: 173mg, Dietary Fiber: 1g, Fat: 20g, Carbs: 7.2g, Protein: 18.2g

Sweet Heat Cheerwine
Baby Back Ribs

Give baby back ribs a twist with sweet heat and serve these for your next backyard barbecue party. Serve with potato salad, baked beans, and crudité veggies for grilling fun.

Servings: 6 – 8
Prep time: 30 minutes
Cook time: 3 hours

2 teaspoons smoked paprika
2 teaspoons chili powder
2 teaspoons dry mustard
1 teaspoon garlic powder
1 teaspoon ground ginger
2 (3 lb.) racks baby back ribs
1 (12-oz.) bottle Cheerwine soft drink
1 (15-oz.) can tomato sauce
1/3 cup light brown sugar
1 tablespoon Dijon mustard
1 teaspoon red chili flakes

1. Preheat oven to 325°F.

2. Combine paprika, chili powder, dry mustard, garlic powder, and ginger in bowl. Sprinkle 2 tablespoons spice mixture over ribs, dividing evenly.

3. Place ribs on a baking sheet; wrap tightly with aluminum foil. Bake 2 hours.

4. Remove foil; rest 30 minutes.

5. Combine Cheerwine, tomato sauce, brown sugar, Dijon mustard, red pepper, and 1 tablespoon spice mixture in a medium saucepan. Bring to a boil over high heat.

6. Reduce heat and simmer, stirring occasionally, until reduced to 2 cups, about 25 to 30 minutes.

7. Heat griddle to medium.

8. Grill ribs, basting with 1 cup of the sauce, turning frequently, until lightly charred and lacquered, about 10 to 15 minutes.

9. Transfer to a platter and serve with remaining sauce.

Nutrition

Calories: 1089, Sodium: 1492mg, Dietary Fiber: 1.5g, Fat: 56.1g, Carbs:76.2g, Protein: 1.3g

Yucatan-Style
Grilled Pork

Elevate simple grilled pork with Yucatan citrus combinations to make something different on your Blackstone Outdoor Griddle Station. Serve this with a side of grilled plantains, veggies, and sparkling water.

Servings: 4
Prep time: 15 minutes
Cook time: 8 minutes

2 pork tenderloins, trimmed
1 teaspoon annatto powder
Olive oil

For the marinade:

2 oranges, juiced
2 lemons, juiced, or more to taste
2 limes, juiced, or more to taste
6 cloves garlic, minced
1 teaspoon ground cumin
1/2 teaspoon cayenne pepper
1/2 teaspoon dried oregano
1/2 teaspoon black pepper

1. Combine marinade ingredients in a mixing bowl and whisk until well-blended.

2. Cut the tenderloins in half crosswise; cut each piece in half lengthwise.

3. Place pieces in marinade and thoroughly coat with the mixture.

4. Cover with plastic wrap and refrigerate 4 to 6 hours.

5. Transfer pieces of pork from marinade to a paper-towel-lined bowl to absorb most of the moisture.

6. Discard paper towels. Drizzle olive oil and a bit more annatto powder on the pork.

7. Preheat grill for medium-high heat and lightly oil.

8. Place pieces evenly spaced on grill; cook 4 to 5 minutes.

9. Turn and grill on the other side another 4 or 5 minutes.

10. Transfer onto a serving platter and allow meat to rest about 5 minutes before serving.

Nutrition

Calories: 439, Sodium: 1382mg, Dietary Fiber: 1.5g, Fat: 33.1g, Carbs:11.4g, Protein: 23.9g

Sweet Smoked
Pork Ribs

Sweet meets smokey and you get none other than ribs that will literally stick to yours! One of my favorite ways to grill ribs, you can serve this with just about anything and it's just plain delicious.

Servings: 8 - 10
Prep time: 30 minutes
Cook time:

10 pounds baby back pork ribs

For the rub:

1 teaspoon liquid smoke, like Colgin

2 tablespoons packed brown sugar

2 tablespoons ground white pepper

2 tablespoons onion powder

1 tablespoon garlic powder

1 tablespoon chili powder

1 tablespoon smoked paprika

1 tablespoon cumin

For the sauce:

1 cup apple juice
1/4 cup packed brown sugar
1/4 cup barbeque sauce

1. Combine rub ingredients in a mixing bowl.
2. Rub the spice mixture into the baby back ribs on all sides.
3. Wrap the ribs well with plastic wrap, and refrigerate for at least 30 minutes prior to cooking.
4. Unwrap baby back ribs and place onto the wire racks of the smoker in a single layer.
5. Combine sauce ingredients in a saucepan and cook for 10 minutes.
6. Grill over indirect medium heat 1 to 1-1/2 hours or until tender.
7. Brush ribs with the glaze and grill, covered, over medium heat 25 to 30 additional minutes or until browned, turning and brushing ribs occasionally with remaining glaze.
8. Serve hot!

Nutrition

Calories: 1329, Sodium: 423mg, Dietary Fiber: 1.2g, Fat: 108.8g, Carbs:10.5g, Protein: 73g

Gremolata
Swordfish Skewers

Delicate, flaky swordfish makes for one delicious grilled skewer! Serve your yummy swordfish with lemon chili pasta, salad, and Chardonnay or sparkling water with lemon.

Servings: 4
Prep time: 20 minutes
Cook time: 10 minutes

1 1/2 lb. skinless swordfish fillet

2 teaspoons lemon zest

3 tablespoons lemon juice

1/2 cup finely chopped parsley

2 teaspoons garlic, minced

3/4 teaspoon sea salt

1/4 teaspoon black pepper

2 tablespoons extra-virgin olive oil, plus extra for serving

1/2 teaspoon red pepper flakes

3 lemons, cut into slices

1. Preheat griddle to medium-high.

2. Combine lemon zest, parsley, garlic, 1/4 teaspoon of the salt, and pepper in a small bowl with a fork to make gremolata and set aside.

3. Mix swordfish pieces with reserved lemon juice, olive oil, red pepper flakes, and remaining salt.

4. Thread swordfish and lemon slices, alternating each, onto the metal skewers.

5. Grill skewers 8 to 10 minutes, flipping halfway through, or until fish is cooked through.

6. Place skewers on a serving platter and sprinkle with gremolata.

7. Drizzle with olive oil and serve.

Nutrition

Calories: 333, Sodium: 554mg, Dietary Fiber: 0.5g, Fat: 16g, Carbs:1.6g, Protein: 43.7g

Spiced Snapper
with Mango & Red Onion Salad

Spiced snapper meats cool, crisp mango salad for one delicious way to grill up lunch. Serve this gorgeous seafood feast with sparkling water with lemon and warm baguettes for a delicious lunch in the sun.

Servings: 4
Prep time: 10 minutes
Cook time: 20 minutes

2 red snappers, cleaned

sea salt

1/3 cup tandoori spice

olive oil, plus more for grill

Extra-virgin olive oil, for drizzling

Lime wedges, for serving

For the salsa:

1 ripe but firm mango, peeled and chopped

1 small red onion, thinly sliced

1 bunch cilantro, coarsely chopped

3 tablespoons fresh lime juice

1. Toss mango, onion, cilantro, lime juice, and a big pinch of salt in a medium mixing bowl; drizzle with a bit of olive oil and toss again to coat.

2. Place snapper on a cutting board and pat dry with paper towels. Cut slashes crosswise on a diagonal along the body every 2" on both sides, with a sharp knife, cutting all the way down to the bones.

3. Season fish generously inside and out with salt. Coat fish with tandoori spice.

4. Preheat griddle medium-high heat and brush with oil.

5. Grill fish for 10 minutes, undisturbed, until skin is puffed and charred.

6. Flip and grill fish until the other side is lightly charred and skin is puffed, about 8 to 12 minutes.

7. Transfer to a platter.

8. Top with mango salad and serve with lime wedges.

Nutrition

Calories: 211 Sodium: 170mg, Dietary Fiber: 2.5g, Fat: 5.4g, Carbs: 18.9g, Protein: 23.6g

Scallops
with Lemony Salsa Verde

Brighten up your grilled scallops with a citrus-infused salsa verde. Lemony salsa verde is the perfect complement to hearty scallops and delicious served alongside risotto or a gorgeous salad.

Servings: 2
Prep time: 10 minutes
Cook time: 5 minutes

1 tablespoon olive oil, plus more for grilling

12 large sea scallops, side muscle removed

Sea salt, for seasoning

For the Lemony Salsa Verde:

½ lemon, with peel, seeded and chopped

5 tomatillos, peeled and pulsed in a blender

1 small shallot, finely chopped

1 garlic clove, finely chopped

¼ cup olive oil

¾ cup finely chopped fresh parsley

½ cup finely chopped fresh cilantro

¼ cup chopped fresh chives

¼ teaspoon sea salt

¼ teaspoon black pepper

1. Toss Lemony Salsa ingredients in a small mixing bowl and set aside.

2. Preheat grill for medium-high and brush with olive oil.

3. Toss scallops with 1 tablespoon olive oil on a baking sheet and season with salt.

4. Add scallops to grill, turning occasionally, until lightly charred and just cooked through, about 2 minutes per side.

5. Serve scallops topped with Lemony Salsa Verde.

Nutrition

Calories: 267, Sodium: 541mg, Dietary Fiber: 3.1g, Fat: 9.6g, Carbs: 13.9g, Protein: 32.4g

Spicy Grilled
Squid

Spice things up with this yummy recipe and serve up some squid at your next dinner party. The perfect appetizer, this is best served on its own or as a decadent appetizer on a bed of leafy greens.

Servings: 4
Prep time: 5 minutes
Cook time: 5 minutes

1 ½ lbs. Squid, prepared
Olive oil

For the marinade:

2 cloves garlic cloves, minced
½ teaspoon ginger, minced
3 tablespoons gochujang
3 tablespoons corn syrup
1 teaspoon yellow mustard
1 teaspoon soy sauce
2 teaspoons sesame oil
1 teaspoon sesame seeds
2 green onions, chopped

1. Preheat griddle to medium high heat and brush with olive oil.
2. Add the squid and tentacles to the griddle and cook for 1 minute until the bottom looks firm and opaque.
3. Turn them over and cook for another minute; straighten out the body with tongs if it curls.
4. Baste with sauce on top of the squid and cook 2 additional minutes.
5. Flip and baste the other side, cook 1 minute until the sauce evaporates and the squid turns red and shiny.

Nutrition

Calories: 292, Sodium: 466mg, Dietary Fiber: 2.7g, Fat: 8.6g, Carbs: 25.1g, Protein: 27.8g

Grilled Oysters
with Spiced Tequila Butter

Tequila infused butter is just the way to elevate oysters fresh off the grill. A delicious appetizer, these oysters are also yummy served with a glass of Sauvignon Blanc or crisp lager and french fries.

Servings: 6
Prep time: 5 minutes
Cook time: 25 minutes

3 dozen medium oysters, scrubbed

Flakey sea salt, for serving

For the butter:

1/4 teaspoon crushed red pepper

7 tablespoons unsalted butter

¼ teaspoon chili oil

1 teaspoon dried oregano

2 tablespoons freshly squeezed lemon juice

2 tablespoons tequila blanco, like Espolon

1. Combine butter ingredients in a small mixing bowl until well-incorporated and set aside.

2. Preheat grill to high.

3. Grill the oysters, flat side up, until they open, about 1 to 2 minutes.

4. Discard the flat top shell and place on a platter; sprinkle with salt flakes.

5. Warm the butter in a microwave for 30 seconds, and spoon the warm tequila butter over the oysters and serve.

Nutrition

Calories: 184, Sodium: 300mg, Dietary Fiber: 0.2g, Fat: 15g, Carbs: 3.8g, Protein: 0.2g

Pop-Open Clams
with Horseradish-Tabasco Sauce

These spicy clams are a great way to serve up some decadent seafood right at home. Best served with crusty grilled bread, you'll love this delicious recipe as a starter or side to the perfect dinner.

Servings: 4
Prep time: 5 minutes
Cook time: 10 minutes

2 dozen littleneck clams, scrubbed

4 tablespoons unsalted butter, softened

2 tablespoons horseradish, drained

1 tablespoon hot sauce, like Tabasco

1/4 teaspoon lemon zest, finely grated

1 tablespoon fresh lemon juice

1/4 teaspoon smoked paprika

Sea salt

1. Preheat the grill to high.
2. Blend the butter with the horseradish, hot sauce, lemon zest, lemon juice, paprika, and pinch of salt.
3. Arrange the clams over high heat and grill until they pop open, about 25 seconds.
4. Carefully turn the clams over using tongs, so the meat side is down.
5. Grill for about 20 seconds longer, until the clam juices start to simmer.
6. Transfer the clams to a serving bowl.
7. Top each with about 1/2 teaspoon of the sauce and serve.

Nutrition

Calories: 191, Sodium: 382mg, Dietary Fiber: 0.3g, Fat: 12.7g, Carbs: 4g, Protein: 14.8g

Spiced
Crab Legs

Crab legs with a twist! If you love spice, you'll love this recipe - but on the chance you just love crab legs you can also substitute chili for olive oil and try it hot and mild!

Servings: 4
Prep time: 5 minutes
Cook time: 5 minutes

1. Preheat grill to high.
2. Brush both sides of crab legs with chili oil and place on grill.
3. Cook 4 to 5 minutes, turning once.
4. Transfer to plates and serve with drawn butter.

4 lbs king crab legs, cooked
2 tablespoons chili oil

Nutrition
Calories: 518, Sodium: 4857mg, Dietary Fiber: 0g, Fat: 13.9g, Carbs: 0g, Protein: 87.1g

Clam Toasts
with Lemon and Green Olives

A Mediterranean delicacy, this bruschetta style dish is just to die for!
Citrus meets tangy for one delicious way to enjoy clams hot off the grill.

Servings: 6 - 8
Prep time: 10 minutes
Cook time: 10 minutes

1 lemon

4 lbs. littleneck clams

1 lemon, sliced

1 garlic clove, minced

1/2 cup parsley, coarsely chopped

1 teaspoon crushed red pepper flakes

1/4 cup olive oil, plus more for drizzling

1 loaf crusty bread, halved lengthwise

1 package Green Olive Tapenade

1 cup shaved Parmesan

Black pepper, to taste,

1. Preheat griddle to medium-high heat.

2. Grill lemon slices, turning occasionally, until lightly charred, about 2 minutes. Transfer to a cutting board and coarsely chop.

3. Place in a medium mixing bowl and set aside.

4. Add clams to grill. Carefully transfer to a large bowl as they open. (Try to save as much clam liquor as possible).

5. Remove clams from their shells and coarsely chop.

6. Transfer clams and liquor to bowl with lemon and add garlic, parsley, red pepper flakes, and oil; fold gently to combine.

7. Drizzle bread with oil and grill, turning halfway through, until toasted and lightly charred, about 5 minutes.

8. Top toasts with 1 teaspoon Green Olive Tapenade, then clam mixture, sprinkle with Parmesan and serve.

Nutrition

Calories: 229, Sodium: 990mg, Dietary Fiber: 1.3g, Fat: 12g, Carbs: 28.9g, Protein: 2.6g

Potato Shrimp
Foil Packets

You can whip up a shrimp boil style meal for a taste of the Bayou right at home with your Blackstone Outdoor Griddle Station. Just be sure to make plenty for the whole family!

Servings: 4
Prep time: 10 minutes
Cook time: 25 minutes

For each Packet:

7 medium sized shrimp, cooked and peeled

3 small red potatoes

1 ear of corn, split in half and shucked clean

2 tablespoons butter

1 tablespoon creole seasoning

1. Preheat the grill to medium-high.

2. Poke the small red potatoes once or twice with a fork, then place them in the microwave for about 3-5 minutes. Place a long piece of foil on your workstation and fold it in half width-wise.

3. Add the foil packet ingredients, and seal foil to make a packet; repeat until 4 packets are made.

4. Place on grill and cook for about 20 minutes or until heated through and the potatoes are done.

5. Carefully remove from the grill and keep foil wrapped tightly until you are ready to tear open and serve.

Nutrition

Calories: 383, Sodium: 1197mg, Dietary Fiber: 3.2g, Fat: 6.4g, Carbs: 29.3g, Protein: 44g

Mexican Shrimp
Tacos

Shrimp tacos are a great way to whip up a healthy dinner in no time for the whole family. These tacos are spiced to perfection and will definitely become a family favorite in no time!

Servings: 4
Prep Time: 10 minutes
Cook Time: 10 minutes

2 lbs. Medium shrimp, peeled and deveined

8 flour tortillas, warmed

1 bag cabbage slaw

1 cup salsa

1 cup Mexican crema

For marinade:

2 tablespoons olive oil

1 tablespoon chili powder

1 tablespoon cumin

1 tablespoon garlic powder

1 tablespoon fresh lime juice

1/4 teaspoon sea salt

1/8 teaspoon fresh ground pepper

1. Preheat a grill to medium-high.

2. Combine oil marinade in a large sealable plastic bag. Add shrimp and toss coat; let marinate in the refrigerator for 30 minutes.

3. Grill shrimp for 3 minutes, on each side, until cooked through.

4. Transfer to a plate.

5. Lay two tortillas on each plate. Evenly divide the shrimp, cabbage slaw, salsa in the middle of each tortilla.

6. Drizzle with Mexican crema and serve.

Nutrition

Calories: 400, Sodium: 92mg, Dietary Fiber: 4g, Fat: 14.7g, Carbs: 30.3g, Protein: 24g

Honey-Lime Tilapia
and Corn Foil Pack

The sweet taste of honey and citrus lime come together to infuse flaky tilapia with a flavor sensation out of this world. Serve these yummy foil packs with garden salads and your favorite sparkling beverage.

Servings: 4
Prep time: 10 minutes
Cook time: 10 minutes

4 fillets tilapia

2 tablespoons honey

4 limes, thinly sliced

2 ears corn, shucked

2 tablespoons fresh cilantro leaves

1/4 cup olive oil

Kosher salt

Freshly ground black pepper

1. Preheat grill to high.

2. Cut 4 squares of foil about 12" long.

3. Top each piece of foil with a piece of tilapia.

4. Brush tilapia with honey and top with lime, corn and cilantro.

5. Drizzle with olive oil and season with sea salt and pepper.

6. Grill until tilapia is cooked through and corn tender, about 15 minutes.

Nutrition

Calories: 319, Sodium: 92mg, Dietary Fiber: 4g, Fat: 14.7g, Carbs: 30.3g, Protein: 24g

Pistachio–Lemon
Pesto Shrimp

Savory pistachios make for one scrumptious pesto marinade when it comes to grilling shrimp. Serve these shrimp as an appetizer or on a bed of orzo drizzled with olive oil for a lovely meal.

Servings: 6
Prep time: 15 minutes
Cook time: 8 minutes

1-1/2 pounds uncooked jumbo shrimp, peeled and deveined

For the pesto:

1/4 cup basil

1/2 cup fresh parsley, chopped

1/3 cup pistachios, shelled

2 tablespoons lemon juice

1 garlic clove, peeled

1/4 teaspoon lemon zest

1/2 cup olive oil

1/4 cup Parmesan cheese, shaved

1/4 teaspoon salt

1/8 teaspoon pepper

1. Add pesto ingredients to a food processor and process until smooth.

2. Transfer 1/3 cup pesto to a large bowl.

3. Fold in shrimp and toss to coat; refrigerate, covered, 30 minutes.

4. Thread shrimp onto metal skewers.

5. Preheat griddle to medium heat.

6. Cook 5-6 minutes, flipping once, until shrimp turn opaque pink.

7. Serve with remaining pesto as a dipping sauce.

Nutrition

Calories: 224, Sodium: 1007mg, Dietary Fiber: 0.6g, Fat: 18.7g, Carbs: 1.6g, Protein: 14.8g

Flaky Grilled
Halibut

Flaky halibut is grilled to perfection in the recipe for the perfect complement to any salad, bed of brown rice, or grilled vegetables from the recipes below. Just be sure to serve this dish with an oaked Chardonnay to really bring out the flavors.

Servings: 4
Prep time: 5 minutes
Cook time: 10 minutes

1 pound fresh halibut filet

For the marinade:

2 tablespoons butter, unsalted and melted

2 tablespoons honey

1/2 lemon, juiced

2 teaspoons Worcestershire sauce

1/2 teaspoon black pepper

2 cloves garlic, minced

1. Combine marinade ingredients in a small mixing bowl.
2. Cut halibut filet into 4 (6 ounce) pieces.
3. Brush both sides of each with the marinade.
4. Preheat griddle to high.
5. Sear the halibut for 90 seconds on each side.
6. Reduce the heat to medium and cook each side for an additional 2-3 minutes, or until the fish can be easily flaked with a fork.

Nutrition

Calories: 250, Sodium: 149mg, Dietary Fiber: 0.3g, Fat: 8.5g, Carbs: 10.5g, Protein: 31g

Salmon Fillets
with Basil Butter & Broccolini

Basil infused broccoli is the perfect way to elevate grilled salmon. Healthy and delicious, this recipe is also easy to make on those busy weeknights when you still want a decadent tasting dinner.

Servings: 2
Prep time: 10 minutes
Cook time: 12 minutes

2 (6 ounce) salmon fillets, skin removed

2 tablespoons butter, unsalted

2 basil leaves, minced

1 garlic clove, minced

6 ounces broccolini

2 teaspoons olive oil

Sea salt, to taste

1. Blend butter, basil, and garlic together until well-incorporated. Form into a ball and place in refrigerator until ready to serve.

2. Preheat griddle to medium-high heat.

3. Season both sides of the salmon fillets with salt and set aside.

4. Add broccolini, a pinch of salt, and olive oil to a bowl, toss to coat, and set aside.

5. Brush griddle with olive oil, and grill salmon for 6 minutes per side for medium.

6. Add the broccolini to the grill, turning occasionally, until slightly charred and golden; about 10-12 minutes.

7. Top each salmon fillet with a slice of basil butter and serve with a side of broccolini.

Nutrition

Calories: 398, Sodium: 303mg, Dietary Fiber: 2.2g, Fat: 26.7g, Carbs: 6.2g, Protein: 35.6g

Basted Dungeness
Crab Legs

Delicate dungeness crab is out of this world when you grill it with a spiced baste. This recipe is sure to capture the heart of any crab lover.

Servings: 4
Prep time: 5 minutes
Cook time: 5 minutes

4 lbs dungeness crab legs, cooked

For the paste:

1/4 cup white wine or white wine vinegar

2 tablespoons sugar

2 tablespoons olive oil

1 tablespoon ginger, minced

1 jalapeno chili, seeded and minced

1 teaspoon, minced garlic

1. Preheat grill to high.
2. Mix baste ingredients together and brush both sides of all crab legs with baste.
3. Cook 4 to 5 minutes, basting often, and turning once.
4. Transfer to plates and serve hot!

Nutrition

Calories: 411, Sodium: 1189mg, Dietary Fiber: 3g, Fat: 13.3g, Carbs: 18.4g, Protein: 54.6g

Spicy Grilled
Jumbo Shrimp

Spicy grilled shrimp is just out of this world! Top your favorite salads, yellow rice and vegetables, or even serve it on its own for grilling fun.

Servings: 6
Prep time: 15 minutes
Cook time: 8 minutes

1-1/2 pounds uncooked jumbo shrimp, peeled and deveined

For the marinade:

2 tablespoons fresh parsley
1 bay leaf, dried
1 teaspoon chili powder
1 teaspoon garlic powder
1/4 teaspoon cayenne pepper
1/4 cup olive oil
1/4 teaspoon salt
1/8 teaspoon pepper

1. Add marinade ingredients to a food processor and process until smooth.
2. Transfer marinade to a large mixing bowl.
3. Fold in shrimp and toss to coat; refrigerate, covered, 30 minutes.
4. Thread shrimp onto metal skewers.
5. Preheat griddle to medium heat.
6. Cook 5-6 minutes, flipping once, until shrimp turn opaque pink.
7. Serve immediately.

Nutrition

Calories: 131, Sodium: 980mg, Dietary Fiber: 0.4g, Fat: 8.5g, Carbs: 1g, Protein: 13.7g

Lobster Tails
with Lime Basil Butter

For one amazing dinner, fire up your Blackstone Outdoor Griddle Station and you can grill up lobster tails in less than 10 minutes. Serve them with grilled vegetables, crab legs, and shrimp for a seafood feast.

Servings: 4
Prep time: 5 minutes
Cook time: 6 minutes

4 lobster tails (cut in half lengthwise)

3 tablespoons olive oil

lime wedges (to serve)

Sea salt, to taste

For the lime basil butter:

1 stick unsalted butter, softened

1/2 bunch basil, roughly chopped

1 lime, zested and juiced

2 cloves garlic, minced

1/4 teaspoon red pepper flakes

1. Add the butter ingredients to a mixing bowl and combine; set aside until ready to use.
2. Preheat griddle to medium-high heat.
3. Drizzle the lobster tail halves with olive oil and season with salt and pepper.
4. Place the lobster tails, flesh-side down, on the grill.
5. Allow to cook until opaque, about 3 minutes, flip and cook another 3 minutes.
6. Add a dollop of the lime basil butter during the last minute of cooking.
7. Serve immediately.

Nutrition

Calories: 430, Sodium: 926mg, Dietary Fiber: 0.5g, Fat: 34.7g, Carbs: 2.4g, Protein: 28g

Coconut Pineapple
Shrimp Skewers

Creamy coconut and fresh pineapple come together to create a taste of Thailand. Serve this decadent shrimp on top a bed of mango sticky rice for one delicious meal.

Servings: 4
Prep time: 1 hour 20 minutes
Cook time: 5 minutes

1-1/2 pounds uncooked jumbo shrimp, peeled and deveined

1/2 cup light coconut milk

1 tablespoon cilantro, chopped

4 teaspoons Tabasco Original Red Sauce

2 teaspoons soy sauce

1/4 cup freshly squeezed orange juice

1/4 cup freshly squeezed lime juice (from about 2 large limes)

3/4 pound pineapple, cut into 1 inch chunks

Olive oil, for grilling

1. Combine the coconut milk, cilantro, Tabasco sauce, soy sauce, orange juice, lime juice. Add the shrimp and toss to coat.
2. Cover and place in the refrigerator to marinate for 1 hour.
3. Thread shrimp and pineapple onto metal skewers, alternating each.
4. Preheat griddle to medium heat.
5. Cook 5-6 minutes, flipping once, until shrimp turn opaque pink.
6. Serve immediately.

Nutrition

Calories: 150, Sodium: 190mg, Dietary Fiber: 1.9g, Fat: 10.8g, Carbs: 14.9g, Protein: 1.5g

Halibut Fillets
with Spinach and Olives

Fresh flaky fish is perfect served with salty olives and fresh spinach. This recipe makes for one quick and easy dinner any day of the week!

Servings: 4
Prep time: 10 minutes
Cook time: 10 minutes

4 (6 ounce) halibut fillets

1/3 cup olive oil

4 cups baby spinach

1/4 cup lemon juice

2 ounces pitted black olives, halved

2 tablespoons flat leaf parsley, chopped

2 teaspoons fresh dill, chopped

Lemon wedges, to serve

1. Preheat griddle to medium heat.
2. Toss spinach with lemon juice in a mixing bowl and set aside.
3. Brush fish with olive oil and cook for 3-4 minutes per side, or until cooked through.
4. Remove from heat, cover with foil and let rest for 5 minutes.
5. Add remaining oil and cook spinach for 2 minutes, or until just wilted. Remove from heat.
6. Toss with olives and herbs, then transfer to serving plates with fish, and serve with lemon wedges.

Nutrition

Calories: 773, Sodium: 1112mg, Dietary Fiber: 1.4g, Fat: 36.6g, Carbs: 2.9g, Protein: 109.3g

Sweet & Smoky
Cedar-Planked Salmon

Grill up restaurant quality meals with this scrumptious recipe with a smoky, sweet flavor that's out of this world.

Servings: 2
Prep time: 2 hrs 5 minutes
Cook time: 30 minutes

2 (6 ounce) salmon fillets, skin on

2 tablespoon light brown sugar

2 teaspoon smoked paprika

1 teaspoon lemon zest

½ teaspoon sea salt

½ teaspoon black pepper

1. Soak a large cedar grilling plank, in water, for 1 to 2 hours.
2. Heat grill to medium.
3. Combine sugar, paprika, lemon zest, salt and pepper in a bowl; season salmon on flesh side.
4. Place salmon on soaked plank, skin side down. Grill, tented with foil, for 25 to 28 minutes for medium.
5. Serve immediately with your favorite sides.

Nutrition
Calories: 267, Sodium: 54 mg, Dietary Fiber: 1g, Fat: 10.8.g, Carbs:10.6g, Protein: 33.4g

CHAPTER

9

Vegetables

& Side Dishes

Tofu Skewers
with Spicy Peanut Sauce

Grilled tofu is the perfect way to enjoy a delicious protein on the grill if you're Vegetarian or Vegan, and it also makes for one lovely side dish. Serve it up on it's own or alongside your favorite grilled vegetables and rice for a healthy meal.

Servings: 8
Prep time: 1 hour
Cook time: 15 minutes

For the grilled tofu skewers:

1 package extra-firm tofu, drained and pressed for 30 minutes or longer

2 tablespoons soy sauce

2 tablespoons water

1 tablespoon honey

1/2 teaspoon smoked paprika

1/2 teaspoon garlic powder

For the spicy peanut sauce:

1/2 cup creamy peanut butter

1/4 cup coconut milk

2 tablespoons soy sauce

2 tablespoons lime juice

1 tablespoon Sriracha

1/4 teaspoon garlic powder

1. Cut the pressed block of tofu into 8 sticks.

2. Add the tofu, soy sauce, water, honey, smoked paprika, and garlic powder to a sealable plastic bag, seal, and toss to coat.

3. Refrigerate for a minimum of 1 hour or 24 hours before grilling.

4. Mix together all of the spicy peanut sauce ingredients in a small mixing bowl; set aside or refrigerate until needed.

5. Before grilling, pour the marinade into a bowl to use as a baste.

6. Thread the tofu onto metal skewers lengthwise.

7. Preheat the griddle to medium-high heat.

8. Grill the skewers for 10 to 15 minutes, turning as needed until char marks form on each side; baste with the leftover marinade often as they cook.

9. Serve hot with the spicy peanut sauce on the side for dipping.

Nutrition

Calories: 138, Sodium: 315mg, Dietary Fiber: 1.3g, Fat: 10.6.g, Carbs: 7.8g, Protein: 5.7g

Cumin Chili
Potato Wedges

Grilled potato wedges are the perfect side dish for sandwiches, burgers, and your favorite proteins. You seriously can't go wrong with this side dish when it comes to making the whole family happy!

Servings: 3 - 4
Prep time: 5 minutes
Cook time: 20 minutes

3 large russet potatoes, scrubbed and cut into 1 inch thick wedges

1/3 cup olive oil

1 teaspoon cumin

1 teaspoon chili powder

1 teaspoon garlic powder

1 teaspoon kosher salt

1 teaspoon freshly ground black pepper

1. Mix together the cumin, chili powder, garlic powder, salt, and pepper in a small bowl and set aside.

2. Preheat one side of the grill to medium-high heat and the other on medium heat.

3. Brush the potatoes all over with olive oil and place over the hot side of the grill and cook until browned and crisp on both sides, about 2 to 3 minutes per side.

4. Move the potatoes to the cooler side of the grill, tent with foil, and continue to grill until cooked through, about 5 to 10 minutes longer.

5. Remove the potatoes from the grill to a large bowl. Sprinkle with the spice mixture and toss to coat.

6. Serve warm and enjoy.

Nutrition

Calories: 343, Sodium: 606mg, Dietary Fiber: 7.1g, Fat: 17.3.g, Carbs: 44.9g, Protein: 5g

Creamy Grilled
Potato Salad

A backyard barbecue favorite, this side compliments any type of meat, fish, or vegetable you grill up.

Servings: 8
Prep Time: 35 minutes
Cook Time: 10 minutes

2 (1.5 lb.) bags baby white potatoes
Non-stick cooking spray

For the dressing:

½ cup mayonnaise

1 tablespoon sour cream

2 teaspoons apple cider vinegar

1 tablespoon fresh parsley, chopped

1 tablespoon fresh basil, chopped

1 teaspoon celery seed

1 tablespoon Dijon mustard

1 tablespoon lemon juice

2 tablespoon olive oil

½ teaspoon sea salt

½ teaspoon black pepper

1. Preheat grill to medium-high, and spray with non-stick cooking spray.

2. Place potatoes on griddle and cook until tender, about 10 minutes.

3. Remove potatoes from grill and allow to cool for 10 minutes.

4. Combine dressing ingredients in a large mixing bowl and whisk until well-combined.

5. Fold in the potatoes until mixed well, and serve at room temperature or well-chilled from the refrigerator overnight.

Nutrition

Calories: 132, Sodium: 246mg, Dietary Fiber: 1.3g, Fat: 8.9.g, Carbs: 13.7g, Protein: 1.9g

Baby Gem Lettuce
with Balsamic & Goat Cheese

Griddle salad is absolutely delicious and an absolute treat to serve with any meal. This side dish is sure to become a family favorite in no time with its robust flavors and creamy goat cheese topping.

Servings: 3
Prep time: 10 minutes
Cook time: 10 minutes

4 Baby Gem lettuce heads, ends trimmed and quartered

3 tablespoon olive oil

1 teaspoon sea salt

1 teaspoon black pepper

3 stalks green onions

1 package soft goat's cheese, crumbled

Balsamic glaze, for serving

1. Preheat the griddle to high heat.
2. Lay cut lettuce and green onion stalks on a baking sheet and coat with olive oil; salt and pepper each evenly.
3. Griddle the vegetables for 1 min per side or until slightly charred. Remove to a plate.
4. Drizzle with balsamic glaze and sprinkle with goat's cheese.
5. Serve warm with your favorite meal!

Nutrition

Calories: 298, Sodium: 751mg, Dietary Fiber: 5.8g, Fat: 20.1.g, Carbs: 28.9g, Protein: 6.2g

Marinated Mushroom
Kabobs

The perfect complement to any grilled meal are grilled vegetable kabobs! Grilled Mushroom Kabobs are seasoned to perfection and will complement any grilled protein or rice dish, too.

Servings: 4
Prep time: 10 minutes
Cook time: 10 minutes

1 punnet white button mushrooms, whole

1 green pepper, deseeded and cut into 2-inch pieces

1 yellow pepper, deseeded and cut into 2-inch pieces

1 onion, cut into 2-inch pieces

1 pint cherry tomatoes

For the marinade:

1/4 cup olive oil

2 cloves garlic, minced

1 lemon, juiced

1/2 teaspoon dried oregano

1/2 teaspoon sea salt

1. Arrange vegetables on metal skewers in an alternating pattern.

2. Place on a baking sheet or piece of aluminum foil.

3. Whisk together the marinade ingredients in a small mixing bowl and pour over skewers; turn skewers to coat well.

4. Preheat a grill to medium heat and cook 4 to 5 minutes on both sides until charred.

5. Remove kabobs to a serving tray and enjoy!

Nutrition

Calories: 173, Sodium: 243mg, Dietary Fiber: 4.2g, Fat: 13.2g, Carbs: 16.1g, Protein: 2.7g

Balsamic Glazed
Veggie Kabobs

Balsamic Glazed Veggie Kabobs are the perfect way to enjoy summer or seasonal vegetables all year around on your Blackstone Outdoor Griddle Station. Don't be afraid to get creative and use yellow squash, butternut squash, parsnips, or sweet potatoes in the fall.

Servings: 4 - 6
Prep time: 10 minutes
Cook time: 8 minutes

½ cup eggplant, cubed into 1-inch chunks

½ cup bell peppers, cubed into 1-inch chunks

½ cup zucchini, cubed into 1-inch chunks

½ cup red onion, cubed into 1-inch chunks

3 tablespoons olive oil

1 teaspoon garlic powder

1 teaspoon sea salt

1 teaspoon black pepper

1/4 cup balsamic glaze

1. Preheat griddle to medium-high heat.

2. Arrange vegetables on metal skewers in an alternating pattern.

3. Place on a baking sheet or piece of aluminum foil.

4. Whisk together the olive oil, garlic powder, salt, and pepper in a small mixing bowl and pour over skewers; turn skewers to coat well.

5. Preheat a grill to medium heat.

6. Brush skewers with balsamic glaze and cook 4 to 5 minutes on both sides until charred; basting with extra glaze often until vegetables are tender.

7. Remove kabobs to a serving tray and enjoy!

Nutrition

Calories: 73, Sodium: 314mg, Dietary Fiber: 0.9g, Fat: 7.1g, Carbs: 3.1g, Protein: 0.5g

Romaine Salad
with Bacon & Blue Cheese

Grilled Romaine with Bacon and Blue Cheese makes for one savory and scrumptious side dish treat. Don't be afraid to serve this one it's own or with grilled chicken breast or leg of lamb for an even more decadent meal.

Servings: 6
Prep time: 5 minutes
Cook time: 15 minutes

3 romaine hearts
12 pieces of thick cut bacon
5 oz blue cheese crumbles

For the dressing:

¼ cup balsamic vinegar
¼ cup light olive oil
¼ teaspoon dried thyme
¼ teaspoon dried parsley
½ teaspoon dried oregano
A little salt and pepper
¼ teaspoon Dijon mustard

1. Preheat the griddle to medium-high heat on one side and high heat on the other

2. Lay the bacon on the medium-high side and griddle for 5 to 8 minutes on each side.

3. Slice each romaine heart in half and set aside.

4. Use a brush to collect a little bit of bacon grease, and brush onto the flat side of each Romaine half.

5. Place the romaine halves flat side down on the high heat side of the grill for 30 seconds each.

6. Remove the bacon to a paper towel lined plate, and chop into crumbles when cool.

7. Remove romaine halves to another plate.

8. Whisk the dressing ingredients together in a small mixing bowl and drizzle over romaine.

9. Top each romaine half with bacon and blue cheese crumbles to serve.

Nutrition

Calories: 283, Sodium: 866mg, Dietary Fiber: 0.6g, Fat: 25.1.g, Carbs: 2.9g, Protein: 12.7g

Potato Salad
with Bacon Vinaigrette

Grilled potato salad is one very decadent side dish! Hearty and full of savory bacon, this salad is the perfect complement to turkey burgers or grilled tofu. Serve it with a glass of sparkling water or white wine, and a grilled baguette to make it a full meal.

Servings: 4
Prep time: 20 minutes
Cook time: 40 minutes

For the potatoes:

7 medium red potatoes, quartered

1 sweet potato, peeled and cut into large chunks

1/4 cup mayonnaise

1 tablespoon dijon mustard

2 teaspoons onion powder

2 teaspoons garlic powder

1/4 teaspoon celery seed

Sea salt, to taste

Freshly ground black pepper, to taste

For the vinaigrette:

2 slices bacon, cooked and chopped

1/4 cup extra-virgin olive oil

2 tablespoons red wine vinegar

2 shallots, minced

2 tablespoons fresh parsley, chopped

1. Preheat a griddle to medium.

2. Put the red potatoes in a large saucepan and cover with cold water by 2 inches. Bring the water to a boil over high heat; after about 10 minutes, add the sweet potatoes.

3. Return to a boil and cook 10 additional minutes.

4. Drain the potatoes and set aside to cool.

5. Whisk the mayonnaise, mustard, onion powder, garlic powder, celery seed, salt and black pepper in medium mixing bowl.

6. Fold the cooled potatoes into the mayonnaise mixture.

7. Mix the vinaigrette ingredients together in a small bowl until well-combined.

8. Use tongs to place the potato pieces back on the hot grill and cook on all sides long enough to cook through and make grill marks, about 1 to 2 minutes per side: be sure to handle the potatoes gently so they don't fall apart.

9. Remove the potatoes from the grill and place in the bowl with the vinaigrette.

10. Gently toss to coat completely and serve warm or cold.

Nutrition

Calories: 521, Sodium: 521mg, Dietary Fiber: 7.7g, Fat: 22.3.g, Carbs: 72.1g, Protein: 12g

A Quick-Start™ Cookbook: COOKING WITH THE BLACKSTONE OUTDOOR GAS GRIDDLE

Artichokes
with Harissa-Honey Dip

Savory, delicate artichokes are just the way to fix up a side dish full of flavor when you pair it with creamy harissa dip. Serve this at your next dinner party or weekend get together for a fun way to enjoy a Mediterranean style side dish with loads of flavor everyone will enjoy.

Servings: 4
Prep time: 10 minutes
Cook time: 30 minutes

4 medium artichokes
1 lemon, juiced
4 tablespoons olive oil

For the Harissa Dip:

1/2 cup mayonnaise
1 tablespoon harissa
1 tablespoon honey
1/4 teaspoon fresh ground pepper
¼ teaspoon sea salt

1. Cut a 1/2 inch off the top of each artichoke, then cut each in half vertically.

2. Trim the pointy ends off the leaves with scissors.

3. Cut out the fuzzy choke in the center of each and discard.

4. Fill a large pot with water and fit with a steaming rack. Place artichokes on rack and steam until they are tender and easily pierced with a fork, about 30 minutes.

5. Set aside to cool for 15 minutes.

6. Preheat grill to high heat.

7. Combine Harissa Dip ingredients in a small mixing bowl until well-combined and set aside.

8. Add lemon and oil to a large mixing bowl, and toss artichokes in lemon and oil.

9. Grill artichokes, cut side down, until nicely charred, about 4 to 5 minutes.

10. Serve hot with harissa dip.

Nutrition

Calories: 328, Sodium: 492mg, Dietary Fiber: 7.4g, Fat: 24.7g, Carbs: 27.7g, Protein: 4.9g

Easy to Make
Grilled Corn

Serve up some hot buttery grilled corn with your next Blackstone Griddle Station meal. This easy side has minimal prep and cook time, so you can enjoy it right alongside your favorite chicken, seafood, pork or beef recipe.

Servings: 8
Prep time: 15 minutes
Cook time: 15 minutes

8 ears corn, shucked and rinsed
1/2 stick butter, unsalted
Sea salt, to taste
Non-stick cooking spray

1. Preheat griddle to medium-high heat for 10 minutes.

2. Spray with non-stick cooking spray and place corn directly on the griddle, turning occasionally, until charred on all sides and fully tender; about 10 minutes total.

3. Remove corn from the griddle and allow to rest for 2 minutes.

4. Roll in butter, sprinkle with salt, and serve warm.

Nutrition

Calories: 183, Sodium: 95 mg, Dietary Fiber: 4.2g, Fat: 7.5.g, Carbs: 29g, Protein: 5.1g

Garlic, Bacon & Lemon
Cauliflower Steaks

Get creative when it comes to adding more veggies to your diet with these yummy grilled cauliflower steaks loaded with flavor! This zesty side will add loads of taste to all of your best grilling recipes above - no matter what your favorite might be.

Servings: 3
Prep time: 15 minutes
Cook time: 15 minutes

2 large heads cauliflower
2 tablespoons olive oil
2 lemons, zested and juiced
2 cloves garlic, finely minced
2 teaspoons sea salt, divided
1/4 teaspoon red pepper flakes
2 slices bacon or turkey bacon, chopped, for garnish
2 scallions, sliced thin, for garnish
Sour cream, for garnish
Lemon wedges, for serving

1. Remove the outer leaves from each cauliflower head. Cut off the stems.
2. Resting the cauliflowers on the stem side, use a large, sharp knife to trim away the sides, then cut the remaining head into 3 thick "steaks" each.
3. Mix the olive oil, lemon zest and lemon juice, garlic, and sea salt, red pepper together in a small mixing bowl.
4. Preheat a grill to medium heat.
5. Brush one side of each cauliflower steak with the lemon olive oil mixture and place seasoned side down on the hot grill.
6. Brush the tops of the steaks with the olive oil mixture.
7. Cook for 5 to 6 minutes, until the bottom is beginning to char. Flip the cauliflower and cook 5 additional minutes, until the cauliflower is tender.
8. Remove from the grill. Garnish with bacon, sour cream, and chives and serve with lemon wedges, if desired.

Nutrition

Calories: 210, Sodium: 1564mg, Dietary Fiber: 5.4g, Fat: 15.1g, Carbs: 17.4g, Protein: 7.7g

Brussels Sprouts
with Balsamic Vinaigrette

Sweet and savory, this side dish is perfect for a busy night when you don't have a lot of time to cook. Ready in just 25 minutes or less, you can whip up a delicious side that compliments your favorite meal or enjoy these on their own with crusty bread or your tastiest soup.

Servings: 4
Prep time: 10 minutes
Cook time: 15 minutes

1 lbs. Fresh brussels sprouts, trimmed and cut in half

1 tablespoon olive oil

sea salt, to taste

black pepper, to taste

Shaved parmesan cheese, for garnish

For the balsamic vinaigrette:

¼ cup balsamic vinegar

1 small clove garlic, minced

1 teaspoon Dijon mustard

1 teaspoon honey

2/3 cup olive oil

1. Preheat your grill to medium high.

2. Toss the brussel sprouts with olive oil, and season with salt and pepper in a large mixing bowl.

3. Grill for 5 to 6 minutes or until the brussel sprouts have nice char marks. Turn the sprouts over and continue to grill for an additional 4 to 5 minutes.

4. Transfer brussel sprouts to a bowl and cover with aluminum foil. This will allow them to steam for a few minutes.

5. Combine all of the balsamic vinaigrette ingredients in a small mixing bowl - except the olive oil; whisk to combine thoroughly.

6. Slowly whisk in the olive oil to create an emulsion.

7. Drizzle the brussel sprouts with the vinaigrette and sprinkle with grated parmesan cheese to serve.

Nutrition

Calories: 97, Sodium: 182mg, Dietary Fiber: 4.4g, Fat: 4.3.g, Carbs: 12.8g, Protein: 4.5g

Greek Grilled
Eggplant

Eggplant is one very versatile vegetable and what better way to enjoy it than Greek-style? You'll fall head over heels with this dish when you pair it with your favorite pasta, seafood, white wine, and sparkling water for a full on Mediterranean meal that is to die for!

Servings: 6
Prep time: 10 minutes
Cook time: 12 minutes

1 medium uncooked eggplant, sliced into twelve ½ inch rounds

crumbled feta cheese, for garnish

For marinade:

2 tablespoons olive oil

2 teaspoons fresh oregano, chopped

1 1/2 teaspoon balsamic vinegar

1/2 teaspoon sea salt

1/8 teaspoon crushed red pepper flakes

1/8 teaspoon garlic powder

1. Preheat grill to medium-high.
2. Combine marinade ingredients in a large mixing bowl.
3. Add eggplant rounds and gently toss to coat.
4. Grill eggplant until lightly charred and tender, about 5 minutes per side.
5. Transfer eggplant to a serving platter.
6. Sprinkle with feta and serve warm with your favorite meal.

Nutrition

Calories: 61, Sodium: 158mg, Dietary Fiber: 2.9g, Fat: 4.9.g, Carbs: 4.9g, Protein: 0.8g

Zucchini & Cauliflower
Skewers with Feta

Serve up something different on the side of your favorite grilling recipes with these yummy Zucchini and Cauliflower Skewers sprinkled with feta. You'll love how decadent you can make your veggies and still eat clean and healthy.

Servings: 4 - 6
Prep time: 5 minutes
Cook time: 10 minutes

2 large zucchini, cut into 1 inch cubes

2 large summer squash, cut into 1 inch cubes

1 head cauliflower, cut into florets

1/4 cup crumbled feta, for garnish

For the marinade:

3 tablespoons olive oil

1 teaspoon sea salt

1 teaspoon black pepper

1 teaspoon garlic powder

1. Preheat grill to medium-high.

2. Skewer zucchini, yellow squash, and cauliflower.

3. Combine marinade ingredients in mixing bowl and coat skewers evenly.

4. Grill, turning occasionally, until vegetables are tender and slightly charred, about 10 to 12 minutes.

5. Transfer to a platter, sprinkle with feta, and serve.

Nutrition

Calories: 115, Sodium: 407mg, Dietary Fiber: 2.9g, Fat: 8.7g, Carbs: 8.4g, Protein: 3.6g

Vegetable Kabobs
with Lemon-Scallion Vinaigrette

Brighten up charred vegetable kabobs with a lemony, tangy vinaigrette.

Servings: 4 - 6
Prep time: 10 minutes
Cook time: 8 minutes

½ cup yellow squash, cubed into 1-inch chunks

½ cup bell peppers, cubed into 1-inch chunks

½ cup zucchini, cubed into 1-inch chunks

½ cup red onion, cubed into 1-inch chunks

½ cup button mushrooms, whole

½ cup cherry tomatoes, whole

3 tablespoons olive oil

1 teaspoon sea salt

1 teaspoon black pepper

For the lemon vinaigrette:

2 scallions, thinly sliced

1 lemon, juiced

1 teaspoon lemon zest

1 tablespoon champagne or white wine vinegar

1 tablespoon olive oil

¼ teaspoon honey

1. Preheat griddle to medium-high heat.
2. Arrange vegetables on metal skewers in an alternating pattern.
3. Place on a baking sheet or piece of aluminum foil.
4. Coat well with olive oil. Season with salt and pepper.
5. Preheat a grill to medium heat.
6. Cook skewers for 4 to 5 minutes on both sides until charred.
7. Combine lemon vinaigrette ingredients in a small mixing bowl and set aside.
8. Remove kabobs to a serving tray, drizzle evenly with lemon vinaigrette, and enjoy!

Nutrition

Calories: 94, Sodium: 316mg, Dietary Fiber: 1.2g, Fat: 7.2g, Carbs: 4.7g, Protein: 0.9g

Parmesan-Garlic

Asparagus

A perfect side dish for any newbie or seasoned griller, Grilled Asparagus cooks up in no time. It's a great way to try one of the other main dish recipes above, and cook a whole meal at once on your Blackstone Outdoor Griddle Station.

Servings: 4-6
Prep time: 5 minutes
Cook time: 10 minutes

1 pound fresh asparagus

2 tablespoons olive oil

3 tablespoons parmesan cheese, shaved

2 garlic cloves, minced

Sea salt, to taste

Black pepper, to taste

1. Preheat griddle to medium high heat.

2. Trim the bottoms off the asparagus.

3. Lay the asparagus on a baking sheet and toss in the olive oil; season with salt and pepper.

4. Add the asparagus to the grill in a row and cook 5 to 10 minutes, until they have char marks and are tender when pierced with a fork.

5. Transfer asparagus to the baking sheet and toss with garlic and parmesan cheese, and serve warm.

Nutrition

Calories: 102, Sodium: 171mg, Dietary Fiber: 1.6g, Fat: 7.8g, Carbs: 3.8g, Protein: 6.2g

Cheesy Ham & Pineapple
Sandwich

Ooey, gooey cheese meets sweet pineapple and ham for one delicious sandwich. Fix these up for a lunch time treat or double the recipe for a family get together for easy fun food to serve on the weekends.

Servings: 4
Prep time: 10 minutes
Cook time: 20 minutes

1 (10 ounce) package deli sliced ham, like Sam's Choice Uncured Honey Ham

4 pineapple rings

4 slices swiss cheese

4 buns, like potato or brioche

Butter, softened, for brushing

Poppy seeds, for brushing

1. Cut a large piece of aluminum foil into four squares, large enough to wrap sandwiches in, and place on a flat work surface.

2. On top of each foil piece, stack a bottom bun, 1/4 of the ham, a pineapple ring, and 1 slice of cheese.

3. Place the top bun on top and brush with melted butter; when all sandwiches are built sprinkle poppy seeds on top.

4. Wrap the sandwiches with foil and leave the top slightly loose.

5. Preheat to medium-high and grill for 20 minutes.

6. Let cool slightly, unwrap, and enjoy!

Nutrition

Calories: 594, Sodium: 3184mg, Dietary Fiber: 0.3g, Fat: 40.3g, Carbs: 4.7g Protein: 47.7g

Garlic Parmesan
Grilled Cheese Sandwiches

Give your grilled cheese a gourmet twist when you elevate them with tangy parmesan cheese. This is my favorite way to enjoy a big bowl of tomato soup or grilled salad found in the recipes above.

Servings: 1
Prep time: 2 minutes
Cook time: 7 minutes

2 slices Italian bread, sliced thin

2 slices provolone cheese

2 tablespoons butter, softened

Garlic powder, for dusting

Dried parsley, for dusting

Parmesan Cheese, shredded, for dusting

1. Spread butter evenly across 2 slices of bread and sprinkle each buttered side with garlic and parsley.

2. Sprinkle a few tablespoons of Parmesan cheese over each buttered side of bread and gently press the cheese into the bread.

3. Preheat the griddle to medium heat and place one slice of bread, buttered side down, into the skillet.

4. Top with provolone slices and second slice of bread with the butter side up.

5. Cook 3 minutes, and flip to cook 3 minutes on the other side; cook until bread is golden and parmesan cheese is crispy.

6. Serve warm with your favorite sides!

Nutrition

Calories: 575, Sodium: 1065mg, Dietary Fiber: 2.8g, Fat: 45.1g, Carbs: 18.1g, Protein: 27.6g

Grilled Cheese
Pizza

Pizza lovers rejoice! You can whip up quick and easy Pizza Grilled Cheese on your Blackstone Outdoor Griddle Station for the whole family in no time.

Servings: 4
Prep Time: 10 minutes
Cook Time: 20 minutes

8 slices French bread
3 tablespoons butter, softened
1/2 cup pizza sauce
1/4 cup mozzarella cheese
1/2 cup pepperoni diced
Garlic powder, for dusting
Oregano, for dusting

1. Spread butter on one side of each French bread slice.
2. Place butter side down on a piece of aluminum foil and dust with garlic powder and oregano.
3. Spread pizza sauce on opposite side of all French bread slices.
4. Top 4 slices of bread with mozzarella cheese, a few slices of pepperoni, and additional mozzarella.
5. Place remaining French bread slices on top of pizza topped bread, butter side up, to create 4 sandwiches.
6. Preheat the griddle to medium heat and place one slice of bread, buttered side down into the skillet.
7. Cook, 3 minutes and flip to cook 3 minutes on the other side; cook until bread is golden and cheese is melted.
8. Serve warm and enjoy!

Nutrition

Calories: 305, Sodium: 664mg, Dietary Fiber: 2.3g, Fat: 12g, Carbs: 40.4g, Protein: 9.4g

Turkey Pesto
Panini

Turkey Pesto Paninis are the perfect quick sandwich to whip up when you are pressed for time. This recipe is delicious served with any soup or salad for one hearty weekday meal or something fun on the weekends.

Servings: 2
Prep time: 5 minutes
Cook time: 6 minutes

1 tablespoon olive oil
4 slices French bread
1/2 cup pesto sauce
4 slices mozzarella cheese
2 cups chopped leftover turkey
1 Roma tomato, thinly sliced
1 avocado, halved, seeded, peeled and sliced

1. Preheat griddle to medium-high heat.
2. Brush each slice of bread with olive oil on one side.
3. Place 2 slices olive oil side down on aluminum foil.
4. Spread 2 tablespoons pesto over 1 side of French bread.
5. Top with one slice mozzarella, turkey, tomatoes, avocado, a second slice of mozzarella, and top with second half of bread to make a sandwich; repeat with remaining slices of bread.
6. Grill until the bread is golden and the cheese is melted, about 2-3 minutes per side.
7. Serve warm with your favorite salad or soup.

Nutrition

Calories: 1129, Sodium: 1243mg, Dietary Fiber: 10g, Fat: 70.9g, Carbs: 53.2g, Protein: 73g

Grilled Veggie
Panini

Hearty and robust, this panini is stuffed with delicious vegetables that really pack a punch. You'll love this hearty sandwich served with carrot sticks and hummus or a bag of kettle chips, and sparkling lemonade or kombucha.

Servings: 4
Prep time: 12 minutes
Cook time: 20 minutes

8 slices sourdough bread

1 small zucchini, cut into strips

1 small yellow squash, cut into strips

1 red bell pepper, cut into strips

1 small red onion, cut into strips

3 basil leaves, chopped

2 teaspoons olive oil

Sea salt, to taste

Pepper, to taste

8 slices provolone cheese

2 tablespoons mayonnaise

1. Preheat entire grill for medium heat.

2. Toss vegetables, olive oil, basil, salt and pepper in a large mixing bowl.

3. Add to the grill and cook 5 minutes, flipping often, until vegetables are softened.

4. Remove from the grill. Top 4 bread slices with mayonnaise, grilled veggies, cheese, and second slice of bread.

5. Place on the griddle and cook for about 3 minutes per side.

6. Remove and serve warm.

Nutrition

Calories: 452, Sodium: 1022mg, Dietary Fiber: 2.7g, Fat: 21g, Carbs: 44g, Protein: 22.8g

Greek Chicken Salad
Pita Pockets

When you need a recipe for leftover grilled chicken, this is the way to go! Otherwise, this recipe is delicious for those who love to meal prep. Just follow a favorite grilled chicken recipe above and you can whip these up in no time.

Servings: 6
Prep time: 10 minutes
Cook time: 5 minutes

1. Whisk together dressing ingredients in a large mixing bowl. Add the sandwich stuffing ingredients to bowl and toss in dressing until well-coated.

2. Fill each pita pocket with Chicken Salad and enjoy!

6 whole wheat pita pockets, halved

For the sandwich stuffing:

1 cup leftover grilled chicken thighs, chopped
4 cups shredded romaine lettuce
1/4 cup chopped grape tomatoes
1/2 cup chopped cucumber
¼ cup black olives, sliced
1/3 cup crumbled feta

For the Greek dressing:

1/4 cup extra-virgin olive oil
2 tablespoons red wine vinegar
1 lemon, juiced
2 cloves garlic, minced
1 teaspoon dried oregano
Sea salt, to taste
Pepper, to taste

Nutrition

Calories: 252, Sodium: 264mg, Dietary Fiber: 4g, Fat: 13.2g, Carbs: 23.8g, Protein: 13.5g

Mini Portobello
Burgers

Delicious and nutritious, these Mini Portobello Burgers are a great animal protein alternative and wonderful for those wanting to add veggies to their healthy lifestyle. Simple and easy, serve them with a side of turnip fries or sweet potato fries for a low-calorie meal.

Servings: 4
Prep time: 15 minutes
Cook time: 15 minutes

4 portobello mushroom caps
4 slices mozzarella cheese
4 buns, like brioche

For the marinade:

1/4 cup balsamic vinegar
2 tablespoons olive oil
1 teaspoon dried basil
1 teaspoon dried oregano
1 teaspoon garlic powder
¼ teaspoon sea salt
¼ teaspoon black pepper

1. Whisk together marinade ingredients in a large mixing bowl. Add mushroom caps and toss to coat.

2. Let stand at room temperature for 15 minutes, turning twice.

3. Preheat grill for medium-high heat.

4. Place mushrooms on the grill; reserve marinade for basting.

5. Grill for 5 to 8 minutes on each side, or until tender.

6. Brush with marinade frequently.

7. Top with mozzarella cheese during the last 2 minutes of grilling.

8. Remove from grill and serve on brioche buns.

Nutrition

Calories: 248, Sodium: 429mg, Dietary Fiber: 2.1g, Fat: 13.5g, Carbs: 20.3g, Protein: 13g

Layered Beef & Corn
Burger

Whip up something different for dinner with this hearty Cornburger!

Servings: 6
Prep time: 20 minutes
Cook time: 30 minutes

1 large egg, lightly beaten

1 cup whole kernel corn, cooked

1/2 cup bread crumbs

2 tablespoons shallots, minced

1 teaspoon Worcestershire sauce

2 pounds ground beef

1 teaspoon salt

1/2 teaspoon pepper

1/2 teaspoon ground sage

1. Combine the egg, corn, bread crumbs, shallots, and Worcestershire sauce in a mixing bowl and set aside.

2. Combine ground beef and seasonings in a separate bowl.

3. Line a flat surface with waxed paper.

4. Roll beef mixture into 12 thin burger patties.

5. Spoon corn mixture into the center of 6 patties and spread evenly across within an inch of the edge.

6. Top each with a second circle of meat and press edges to seal corn mixture in the middle of each burger.

7. Grill over medium heat, for 12-15 minutes on each side or until thermometer reads 160° F and juices run clear.

Calories: 354, Sodium: 578mg, Dietary Fiber: 1.2g, Fat: 11.1g, Carbs: 12.3g, Protein: 49.1g

Pork Tenderloin
Sandwiches

Tender grilled pork is the perfect way to grill up a savory sandwich on your Blackstone Outdoor Griddle Station. This simple, yet flavorful sandwich will have you grilling like a gourmet chef in no time.

Servings: 6
Prep time: 10 minutes
Cook time: 25 minutes

2 (3/4-lb.) pork tenderloins
1 teaspoon garlic powder
1 teaspoon sea salt
1 teaspoon dry mustard
1/2 teaspoon coarsely ground pepper
Olive oil, for brushing
6 whole wheat hamburger buns
6 tablespoons barbecue sauce

1. Stir the garlic, salt, pepper, and mustard together in a small mixing bowl.

2. Rub pork tenderloins evenly with olive oil, then seasoning mix.

3. Preheat grill to medium-high heat, and cook 10 to 12 minutes on each side or until a meat thermometer inserted into thickest portion registers 155° F.

4. Remove from grill and let stand 10 minutes.

5. Slice thinly, and evenly distribute onto hamburger buns.

6. Drizzle each sandwich with barbecue sauce and serve.

Nutrition

Calories: 372, Sodium:694 mg, Dietary Fiber: 2.9g, Fat: 13.4g, Carbs: 24.7g, Protein: 37.2g

Prosciutto Pesto
Hot Dog

These gourmet hot dogs will knock your socks off! Just be sure to pair them with gourmet kettle chips, a grilled salad from the recipes above, and an ice cold craft beer or your favorite soft drink.

Servings: 4
Prep time: 15 minutes
Cook time: 15 minutes

4 smoked turkey hot dogs, like Oscar Meyer Uncured Turkey Dogs

4 large hot dog buns or split top hoagies

6 ounces fresh mozzarella cheese

1/3 cup pesto, divided

3 ounces prosciutto, sliced thinly

¼ cup marinate artichoke hearts, chopped

Olive oil, for drizzling

Parmesan cheese, shaved for garnish

1. Preheat the entire grill to medium heat.

2. Add hot dogs, to one side, and reduce that side's heat to low. Grill until cooked through; about 5 to 7 minutes; turning occasionally.

3. Fry the sliced prosciutto until crispy on the other side of the griddle; about 3 minutes. Drain on a paper towel lined plate; and set aside.

4. In the last minute on the grill, top the hot dogs with thin slices of the mozzarella cheese, and remove once the cheese is melted.

5. Toast the buns on the griddle for 2 minutes and remove.

6. Spread pesto onto the toasted buns.

7. Top with mozzarella covered hot dog.

8. Top with crispy prosciutto, artichoke hearts, parmesan cheese and a drizzle of olive oil.

9. Serve immediately!

Nutrition

Calories: 457, Sodium: 1166mg, Dietary Fiber: 1.5g, Fat: 25.8g, Carbs: 26.3g, Protein: 29.9g

Curry Pork Wraps

with Nectarine Chutney

Curried pork is a delicious way to enjoy your Blackstone Outdoor Griddle Stations - especially when you use it to stuff luscious wraps for one mouthwatering way to enjoy lunch or dinner.

Servings 3 - 6
Prep time: 2 hrs 10 minutes
Cook time: 25 minutes

1 (3/4 lb.) pork tenderloin
6 wheat tortillas
cucumber slices, for serving
red onion slices, for serving
baby spinach, for serving

For the marinade:
1 cup Greek yogurt, plain
3 tablespoon lime juice
2 tablespoon mild yellow curry powder
1 teaspoon cumin
1/2 teaspoon pepper
1/2 teaspoon salt
1/4 teaspoon ground nutmeg

For Nectarine Chutney:
2 cups nectarines, chopped
1/3 cup mango chutney
2 tablespoon apple cider vinegar
2 tablespoon fresh cilantro, chopped
2 tablespoon fresh mint, chopped
1/2 teaspoon salt
1/2 teaspoon pepper

1. Combine marinade ingredients in a large mixing bowl.
2. Cut 4 (1-inch) slits into the pork tenderloin. Add pork to marinade, turning to coat, cover and marinate in the refrigerator for 2 to 24 hours.
3. Combine chutney ingredients in a bowl; cover and refrigerate until ready to assemble wraps.
4. Remove pork from marinade.
5. Preheat grill to medium-high heat, and cook 10 to 12 minutes on each side or until a meat thermometer inserted into thickest portion registers 155° F.
6. Remove from grill and let stand 10 minutes.
7. Slice pork thinly. Layer a tortilla with slices of pork, baby spinach, cucumber slices, red onion and a dollop of nectarine chutney.
8. Serve immediately and enjoy.

Nutrition

Calories: 248, Sodium: 516mg, Dietary Fiber: 10g, Fat: 5.3g, Carbs: 28.6g, Protein: 22.4g

Bacon Jalapeno
Wraps

When bacon meets jalapeno you have a flavor explosion from out of this world! Serve these delicious spicy wraps at your next family get together or tailgate party with cool veggies like carrot and celery sticks on the side.

Servings: 4
Prep time: 5 minutes
Cook time: 10 minutes

1 package bacon, uncured and nitrate free

6 fresh jalapeno peppers, halved lengthwise and seeded

1 (8 ounce) package cream cheese

1 dozen toothpicks, soaked

1. Preheat an outdoor grill for high heat.
2. Fill jalapeno halves with cream cheese.
3. Wrap each with bacon. Secure with a toothpick.
4. Place on the grill, and cook until bacon is crispy, about 5 to 7 minutes per side.
5. Remove to a platter to cool and serve warm.

Nutrition

Calories: 379, Sodium: 1453mg, Dietary Fiber: 0.9g, Fat: 33.4g, Carbs: 3.5g, Protein: 16.3g

Sun-Dried Tomato
and Chicken Flatbreads

*Grilled chicken flatbreads are a perfect afternoon snack or lunch option.
Serve with a salad for a full meal, or enjoy as-is with friends and family
on a sunny afternoon. Delicious paired with sparkling water.*

Servings: 4
Prep time: 5 minutes
Cook time: 7 minutes

4 flat breads or thin pita bread

For the topping:

**1 1/2 cups of sliced grilled
chicken, pre-cooked or
leftovers**

**1/2 cup sun-dried tomatoes,
coarsely chopped**

**6 leaves fresh basil, coarsely
chopped**

**3 cups mozzarella cheese,
shredded**

1 teaspoon salt

1 teaspoon ground black pepper

1 teaspoon red pepper flakes

Olive or chili oil, for serving

1. Preheat the griddle to low heat.

2. Mix all the topping ingredients together in a large mixing bowl with
   a rubber spatula.

3. Lay flatbreads on griddle, and top with an even amount of topping
   mixture; spreading to the edges of each.

4. Tent the flatbreads with foil for 5 minutes each, or until cheese is
   just melted.

5. Place flatbreads on a flat surface or cutting board, and cut each
   with a pizza cutter or kitchen scissors.

6. Drizzle with olive or chili oil to serve!

Nutrition

Calories: 276, Sodium: 1061 mg, Dietary Fiber: 1.9g, Fat: 5.7g, Carbs: 35.7g, Protein: 19.8g

Veggie Pesto
Flatbread

Grilled Veggie Pesto Flatbreads are simply perfect for any weekend or party with family and friends. When it comes to having vegetarian options for everybody, this is a great way to create a special sharing flatbread so everyone is included in the grilling fun.

Servings: 4
Prep time: 40 minutes
Cook time: 10 minutes

2 prepared flatbreads
1 jar pesto
1 cup shredded mozzarella cheese

For the topping:

1/2 cup cherry tomatoes, halved
1 small red onion, sliced thin
1 red bell pepper, sliced
1 yellow bell pepper, sliced
1/2 cup mixed black and green olives, halved
1 small yellow squash or zucchini, sliced
2 teaspoon olive oil
¼ teaspoon sea salt
¼ teaspoon black pepper

1. Preheat the griddle to low heat.
2. Spread an even amount of pesto onto each flatbread.
3. Top with ½ cup mozzarella cheese each.
4. Mix all the topping ingredients together in a large mixing bowl with a rubber spatula.
5. Lay flatbreads on griddle, and top with an even amount of topping mixture; spreading to the edges of each.
6. Tent the flatbreads with foil for 5 minutes each, or until cheese is just melted.
7. Place flatbreads on a flat surface or cutting board, and cut each with a pizza cutter or kitchen scissors.
8. Serve warm!

Nutrition

Calories: 177, Sodium: 482mg, Dietary Fiber: 1.7g, Fat: 11.9g, Carbs: 12.6g, Protein: 5.5g

Grilled Vegetable
Pizza

Grilled Vegetable Pizzas are a great weeknight treat or a way to use the summer vegetables in your garden. Just be sure to get creative with your toppings and you'll really savor this delicious grilled pizza.

Servings: 6
Prep time: 30 minutes
Cook time: 10 minutes

8 small fresh mushrooms, halved

1 small zucchini, cut into 1/4-inch slices

1 small yellow pepper, sliced

1 small red pepper, sliced

1 small red onion, sliced

1 tablespoon white wine vinegar

1 tablespoon water

4 teaspoons olive oil, divided

1/2 teaspoon dried basil

1/4 teaspoon sea salt

1/4 teaspoon pepper

1 prebaked, 12-inch thin whole wheat pizza crust

1 can (8 ounces) pizza sauce

2 small tomatoes, chopped

2 cups shredded part-skim mozzarella cheese

1. Preheat a grill to medium-high heat.

2. Combine mushrooms, zucchini, peppers, onion, vinegar, water, 3 teaspoons oil and seasonings in a large mixing bowl.

3. Transfer to grill and cook over medium heat for 10 minutes or until tender, stirring often.

4. Brush crust with remaining oil and spread with pizza sauce.

5. Top evenly with grilled vegetables, tomatoes and cheese.

6. Tent with aluminum foil and grill over medium heat for 5 to 7 minutes or until edges are lightly browned and cheese is melted.

7. Serve warm!

Nutrition

Calories: 111, Sodium: 257mg, Dietary Fiber: 1.7g, Fat: 5.4g, Carbs: 12.2g, Protein: 5g

Cornbread
with Jalapeño Honey Butter

Hot off the grill this cornbread is delicious and best served alongside your favorite soups or pot of southern style beans. Savory flavor meets spicy sweet for a genuinely delicious combination you're bound to love cooking up.

Servings: 6
Prep time: 5 minutes
Cook time: 5 minutes

1 loaf of cornbread, prepared
1/2 cup salted butter, softened
1 jalapeno pepper, seeded and minced
2 tablespoons raw honey

1. Slice prepared cornbread into squares and split each square horizontally; set aside.
2. Add remaining ingredients to a medium mixing bowl and beat until butter is creamy.
3. Spread the butter on split sides of cornbread squares.
4. Grill cornbread over medium-high heat, about 3 minutes on each side, or until cornbread is crispy and has grill-marks.
5. Serve immediately.

Nutrition

Calories: 189, Sodium: 187mg, Dietary Fiber: 0.3g, Fat: 16.4g, Carbs: 10.7g, Protein: 0.9g

Charred Bread
with Ricotta and Cherry Salsa

Ricotta and cherries are the perfect topping for chargrilled bread. Enjoy this bread as an appetizer for a dinner party or the perfect dessert with wine after a romantic dinner.

Servings: 6
Prep time: 10 minutes
Cook time: 5 minutes

1 baguette, sliced in half lengthwise

5 tablespoons fresh lemon juice

12 ounces fresh cherries, pitted and cut into 1/3-inch-thick slivers

½ cup olive oil, plus more for brushing

12 ounces whole-milk fresh ricotta

Flaky sea salt, for garnish

1. Add lemon juice, cherries, and olive oil to a mixing bowl and toss to coat.

2. Preheat grill to medium-low heat.

3. Brush cut sides of baguette with oil.

4. Grill, cut sides down, until bread is toasted and golden brown, about 3 minutes.

5. Let bread cool for 1 minute, then spread generous amounts of ricotta over both pieces.

6. Cut each half on a diagonal into 6 pieces.

7. Arrange on a plate and top with cherry salsa.

8. Sprinkle lightly with sea salt, and enjoy.

Nutrition

Calories: 177, Sodium: 482mg, Dietary Fiber: 1.7g, Fat: 11.9g, Carbs: 12.6g, Protein: 5.5g

CHAPTER

11

Desserts

Peach & Berry
Dessert Pizza

Grilled peaches make the perfect sweet treat to top a pizza, and you can whip this delicious dessert up in no time. Serve it at a dinner party with friends or as a scrumptious treat just for yourself.

Servings 2 - 4
Prep time: 5 minutes
Cook time: 10 minutes

¼ package cream cheese, softened

1 (8-ounce) package crème fraîche

3 tablespoons honey

¼ teaspoon fresh orange zest

1 tablespoon fresh orange juice

1/8 teaspoon ground cinnamon

1 (1 lb.) package refrigerated pizza dough

1 peach, halved, pitted

1 cup blackberries

1 cup raspberries

Mint leaves, torn, as garnish

Honey, as garnish

Olive oil, for grill

1. Preheat grill to high heat.

2. Beat cream cheese until smooth in a medium mixing bowl.

3. Fold in crème fraîche, honey, orange zest, orange juice, and cinnamon, and beat until well-combined; refrigerate until ready to use.

4. Stretch or roll dough to a 12-inch circle.

5. Brush preheated grill with oil. Place dough on grill. Tent with foil and cook until crispy, approximately 2 to 3 minutes per side.

6. Remove from grill and set aside.

7. Place peach halves, cut sides down, on grill and cook until softened; about 2 to 3 minutes. Cut into slices.

8. Spread crème fraîche mixture onto warm crust. Top with peach slices, blackberries, and raspberries. Garnish with torn mint, and drizzle with honey.

9. Cut into slices and serve immediately.

Nutrition

Calories: 799, Sodium: 595mg, Dietary Fiber: 8.6g, Fat: 52.7g, Carbs: 74.9g, Protein: 10g

Pound Cake
with Espresso Chocolate Sauce

Delicious pound cake is turned into a grilled delicacy covered in luscious espresso chocolate sauce in this griddle recipe. If you love decadent desserts, this recipe is just right for your sweet tooth.

Servings: 8
Prep time: 15 minutes
Cook time: 8 minutes

2 tablespoons boiling water

1 tablespoon instant espresso coffee powder

3/4 cup whipping cream

1 tablespoon light-color corn syrup

1 1/3 cup special dark baking chocolate

1 (16 ounce) pound cake

2 tablespoons orange juice

2 tablespoons orange liqueur

1 cup whipped cream, like TruWhip

1/2 cup pistachio nuts, chopped

1. Combine boiling water and espresso powder in a small mixing bowl; set aside.

2. Combine the 3/4 cup whipping cream and the corn syrup in a heavy saucepan and bring to a boil.

3. Remove from heat and stir in espresso mixture; add chocolate all at once. Cover and let mixture stand for 4 minutes.

4. Whisk until chocolate is melted and mixture is smooth and cover to keep warm.

5. Cut the pound cake into eight 3/4-inch-thick slices.

6. Poke holes in each slice several times with a fork.

7. Mix orange juice and orange liqueur together in a small mixing bowl.

8. Drizzle orange juice mixture evenly over cake slices.

9. Preheat the grill to medium-high heat. Grill cake for 2 to 4 minutes on each side, until toasted and heated through.

10. Serve grilled cake slices with whipped cream, pistachio nuts, and chocolate sauce.

Nutrition

Calories: 305 Sodium: 221mg, Dietary Fiber: 0.6g, Fat:14.2g, Carbs: 38.5g, Protein: 3g

Mint Julep
Peaches

Serve up a taste of the south at your next dinner party when you grill up some delicious mint julep style peaches. Just the right amount of sweet, these peaches are great served with an after dinner cocktail or dessert wine.

Servings: 4
Prep time: 10 minutes
Cook time: 10 minutes

4 ripe peaches

½ cup shortening

½ cup Kentucky Bourbon, like Maker's Mark

2 cups dark brown sugar, packed

4 sprigs mint, stems separated

2 cups vanilla bean ice cream

1. Preheat grill to high.

2. Combine bourbon, brown sugar, and mint stems in a small saucepan over medium heat. Allow sauce to reduce for 5 minutes.

3. Halve peaches & remove the stones.

4. Brush the flesh evenly with shortening.

5. Grill peaches, shortening side down, and tented with foil for 2 minutes.

6. Rotate 180 degrees and grill, covered for an additional 2 minutes.

7. Plate peaches, flesh side up, and drizzle with glaze. Top with ice cream and garnish with fresh mint leaves.

Nutrition

Calories: 761, Sodium: 54mg, Dietary Fiber: 3.1g, Fat: 36.1g, Carbs: 105.1g, Protein: 3.9g

Pound Cake
with Sour Cherry Syrup

Grilled Pound Cake can be just as decadent when topped with fruit for dessert, too! This quick and easy dessert will have all your friends asking for your recipe after your next Sunday Brunch or decadent dinner party.

Servings: 12
Prep time: 10 minutes
Cook time: 11 minutes

11/3 lb. fresh cherries
3/4 cup sugar
4 tablespoons sea salt
1 cup sour cream
2 tablespoons brown sugar, packed
1/2 teaspoon fresh lemon juice
1 pound cake, cut into 8 slices

1. Bring cherries, sugar, 1/4 cup water, and salt to a boil in a medium saucepan on medium heat.
2. Cook, stirring occasionally, until a syrup forms, about 10 minutes. Let cool.
3. Preheat grill to medium heat.
4. Mix sour cream, brown sugar, and lemon juice in a small mixing bowl, and chill until ready to serve.
5. Grill pound cake for 1 minute per side.
6. Transfer pound cake to plates and top each slice with a dollop of sour cream mixture and 1/3 cup cherry syrup.

Nutrition

Calories: 394, Sodium: 2038mg, Dietary Fiber: 0.9g, Fat: 9.6g, Carbs: 75.8g, Protein: 2.4g

Grilled Watermelon
with Yogurt

If you like watermelon and feta, you'll love this watermelon grilled with a creamy twist! The perfect after school or work snack - this recipe doesn't have to be served as dessert. You can enjoy it anytime of the day.

Servings: 6
Prep time: 5 minutes
Cook time: 10 minutes

1 cup plain Greek yogurt

2 tablespoons freshly squeezed lemon juice

1 tablespoon white wine vinegar

1 teaspoon coarsely chopped thyme

1 tablespoon extra-virgin olive oil, plus more for drizzling

Twelve 3-inch-long triangles of seedless red watermelon, about 1 inch thick

Sea salt, for seasoning

1/4 cup small mint leaves

Honey, for drizzling

1. Preheat griddle to high heat.

2. Combine yogurt, lemon juice, vinegar, thyme and the 1 tablespoon of olive oil in a small mixing bowl.

3. Drizzle the watermelon triangles with olive oil and season with salt.

4. Grill over high heat until charred, about 1 minute per side; transfer to plates.

5. Top the watermelon with the yogurt sauce and season with black pepper.

6. Garnish with mint and honey drizzle to serve.

Nutrition

Calories: 126, Sodium: 97mg, Dietary Fiber:1.3g, Fat:2.7g, Carbs: 22.8, Protein: 5.3g

Pineapple
with Cinnamon Honey Drizzle

Grilled pineapple is the perfect after dinner treat when drizzled with honey and cinnamon. This is one healthy recipe the whole family will absolutely adore!

Servings 6
Prep Time 10 minutes
Cook Time 6 minutes

1 pineapple sliced into spears
1/2 cup honey
1 teaspoon cinnamon
Pinch of nutmeg
Non-stick cooking spray

1. Preheat griddle to medium heat and spray with non-stick cooking spray.

2. Add pineapple slices and cook 3 minutes on each side.

3. Microwave honey in a glass bowl for 30 seconds.

4. Fold in the cinnamon and nutmeg.

5. Drizzle the grilled pineapple with the honey and serve warm.

Nutrition

Calories: 101, Sodium: 2mg, Dietary Fiber: 0.7g, Fat: 0.1g, Carbs: 27.2g, Protein: 0.3g

S'mores
Hand Pies

When you don't have time to build a fire, you will have time to whip up some s'mores on your Blackstone Outdoor Griddle. Simple to assemble, these delicious treats can be cooked in no time - and everyone will fall head over heels for the delicious taste of s'mores.

Servings: 4
Prep time: 10 minutes
Cook time: 5 minutes

1 package pie crust dough
12 milk chocolate candy bar, like Hershey's
1 graham cracker split into four segments
1/2 cup marshmallow cream
40 mini marshmallows
1 egg white, beaten

1. Roll out the pie crust dough and cut it into four large circles, about 6 inches each, using a bowl as a pattern.
2. Place one graham cracker segment in the center of the dough circle.
3. Add two squares of chocolate and a teaspoon of marshmallow cream.
4. Add about ten mini marshmallows on top of the marshmallow cream.
5. Wet the edges of the dough with water using your finger, and fold the dough over the s'mores toppings, pressing it in place.
6. Fold up the edges, pressing them in place.
7. Crimp the edges with a fork to seal.
8. Brush the whole hand pie, top and bottom, with egg white.
9. Preheat the griddle to medium heat.
10. Lightly grease the griddle with non-stick cooking spray.
11. Cook the hand pies on each side for 2 minutes.
12. Then, cook on each side an additional minute - but keep an eye on them as they can burn.
13. Remove from the grill and add a dab of marshmallow cream to the top of each hand pie.
14. Stick a piece of chocolate bar in the middle of the marshmallow cream to hold it in place, and serve warm.

Nutrition

Calories: 899, Sodium: 341mg, Dietary Fiber: 4.9g, Fat: 49.9g, Carbs: 99.6g, Protein: 12.7g

44057222R00098

Made in the USA
Lexington, KY
06 July 2019